Refle
of
Broken Son

For hearts that long to hope again

Alister Hooke

Reflections of a Broken Son

Copyright © Alister Hooke 2020

All rights reserved. No part of this publication may be reproduced, stored in a retrieval system, or transmitted in any form by any means, electronic, mechanical, photocopying or otherwise, without the prior written consent of the publisher. Short extracts may be used for review purposes.

ISBN: 978-1-914173-02-8

Scripture quotations have been taken from:

- *THE MESSAGE, copyright* © 1993, 1994, 1995, 1996, 2000, 2001, 2002, by Eugene H. Paterson, used by permission of NavPress. All rights reserved. Represented by Tyndale House Publishers Inc.
- Holy Bible, New International Version® Anglicized, NIV® Copyright © 1979, 1984, 2011 by Biblica, Inc.® Used by permission. All rights reserved worldwide.
- New Living Translation, copyright ©1996, 2004, 2015 by Tyndale House Foundations. Used by permission of Tyndale House Publishers, Inc., Carol Stream, Illinois 60188. All rights reserved.

You can contact Alister at: alisterhooke59@yahoo.co.uk

Dedication

To my wife Lesley and three children, Rachel, Emma and David.
You guys are the most amazing people I know on earth, and I cannot express how profoundly happy I am to co-exist with you. Except that I just have!

Acknowledgements

Lesley – you are my rock and the steady influence in my turbulent life. Thank you for encouraging me to keep on writing. Your trust and patience have not been lost on me. Thanks to Rachel, Emma and David for letting me use their names in this book about their dad's life journey; also, for being my constant muse and support during this difficult coronavirus lockdown. Love you as always.

Thanks to Alec, Arfan, Carolyn, Denise, Ian, Irene, James, Laura, Margaret and Stuart for reviewing the first draft of this book and giving me such positive feedback, as well as constructive criticism. As a result of your efforts, key changes and additions were made. Your impressions are in the fabric of this final output. Much appreciated, folks.

Finally, I want to mention three special people: Gwen, Bill and Ian. I met these three people (in that order) at critical points of my life when I was unravelling and falling into chaos. Their inputs into my life were timely and extraordinary. Without their respective life-saving interventions, it is no exaggeration to say that I would not have written this book. As I live and breathe, thank you from my heart.

Note About The Title Page Illustration

According to Wikipedia, *kintsugi* (golden joinery), also known as *kintsukuroi* (golden repair), is the Japanese art of repairing broken pottery by mending the breakages with a lacquer that has been dusted or mixed with powdered gold. Silver or platinum can also be used. As a philosophy, breakage and repair are perceived as crucial and integral components of an object's story, not something to disguise or put out of sight.

After viewing countless images of vases and plates with gleaming golden veins streaked across their mended surfaces, I envisioned a statuette of a man being subject to similar treatment. For the picture I had in mind, the man was naked – stripped of guile and self-made attempts at concealment – and reaching out to God for help. Like broken pottery submitted to the process of *kintsugi,* the broken man had been touched by God (*the golden presence of the divine*) never to be the same again. And like mended pottery, his self-evident brokenness was not on display to invite criticism or contempt, but rather to point to the craftsmanship of a loving Father in heaven who delights in healing the broken-hearted.

Abbreviations used in this book

1 Chron.	1 Chronicles	**Heb.**	Hebrews
1 Cor.	1 Corinthians	**Isa.**	Isaiah
1 Pet.	1 Peter	**Jer.**	Jeremiah
1 Sam.	1 Samuel	**Josh.**	Joshua
1 Thess.	1 Thessalonians	**Judg.**	Judges
1 Tim.	1 Timothy	**Lam.**	Lamentations
2 Cor.	2 Corinthians	**Matt.**	Matthew
2 Pet.	2 Peter	**Mic.**	Micah
2 Sam.	2 Samuel	**Num.**	Numbers
2 Tim.	2 Timothy	**Phil.**	Philemon
Col.	Colossians	**Prov.**	Proverbs
Deut.	Deuteronomy	**Ps.**	Psalms
Eph.	Ephesians	**Rev.**	Revelations
Exo.	Exodus	**Rom.**	Romans
Ezek.	Ezekiel	**Song**	Song of Solomon
Gal.	Galatians	**Zech.**	Zechariah
Gen.	Genesis		

Bible Translations:

MSG	The Message
NIVUK	New International Version (UK)
NLT	New Living Translation

Commendations

I *LOVED* this book! It is engaging, personal and, most importantly, from the heart. It's a book that you can read and appreciate whether you're Christian or non-Christian, and I think that's just wonderful. To me, it's a book about hope. Alister's use of imagery throughout is fantastic. A definite must-read!

Denise Russell
Mother, Sister, Friend, Carer

It has been my great privilege to know Alister for over 20 years and, in that time, I have watched him recognise, process and move on from his past life experiences, maturing into a godly man, a good husband and a wonderful father. I would heartily recommend this book to you in which he shares his story and also the revelations discovered on that journey, which, in his own words, 'turned his world upside down'.

Margaret Peat
Author, Speaker, Pastor's Wife

Hooked from page one. What a privilege to walk alongside Alister on his journey from darkness to light. For someone like myself whose religious upbringing is fair-weather to say the least, Alister has been able to open up a new genre to me that I never considered as relevant to my life. Thank you and I look forward to the next chapter of your literary journey as you continue to walk your life's path.

Carolyn Oxenham
Friend, Part-time Christian

In this book, Alister shares in an authentic and refreshing way his personal journey into finding freedom and hope. Those who have suffered or are suffering from anxiety, low self-esteem,

Reflections of a Broken Son

identity struggles, addiction, perfectionism and/or loneliness will relate to the battles fought and won within these pages. If you allow yourself to be open and real with God as you journey through Alister's book, and apply the lessons that God has shown him, my prayer is that you may know the transformative power of God, just as Alister has.

Rev. James Richardson
Friend, Pastor

Reading this remarkable book provided a fascinating perspective on a lifelong journey in search of meaning amidst the pitfalls of modern life. As a non-Christian, I still found many valuable life lessons that could be gleaned from this work, both spiritual and more down-to-earth. Replete with both good humour and deep insight, this book is a must-read, particularly for those searching for a contemporary perspective on the reality of grace.

Arfan Iqbal
Friend, Professional Researcher

Reflections of a Broken Son is a book written for those of us who can own the title, and that's more people than you would think. A book honestly considering the paths that we often follow (a bit like the yellow brick road), heading for a destination that we don't always know where it actually is. A book about struggle, challenge and turmoil, but ultimately about love, hope and redemption. A book written for those of faith and none; but ultimately about humanity and its journey… with a twist… we don't have to do it alone. There is a destination. Read on!

Alec Keys
Company Director, MBA, CIOB, Broken Son

Contents

Foreword		11
Introduction		13
Chapter 1	Humpty Dumpty	15
Chapter 2	Freefalling	21
Chapter 3	The Big Picture	29
Chapter 4	The Father's Promise	37
Chapter 5	In His Hands	49
Chapter 6	Death of a Superhero	67
Chapter 7	Turning Up the Heat	85
Chapter 8	Coming Out From the Trees	103
Chapter 9	The Path of Sonship	125
Chapter 10	From Here to Eternity	145
Twelve Questions for Reflection		151
Afterword for Those Affected by Book		175

Reflections of a Broken Son

Foreword

Every aspect of *Reflections of a Broken Son* is derived from the personal experience of a gentle and humble man. Alister Hooke's life journey from brokenness and despair to wholeness and hope is powerfully portrayed in this gem. The three sections in the book – life experience, theological teaching and self-reflection – are addressed with equal sincerity, and there is an intelligent flow throughout.

Alister's powerful story is peppered with memories, reflections, ordinary and supernatural events, and each experience is described with honesty, authenticity and humour. (I loved the asides!) Mental wellbeing is a hot topic for churches today and I applaud his boldness in taking the issue seriously. He doesn't sugar-coat the struggles faced by Christians and offers thoughtful, well-researched resources to help the reader understand and address their own emotional and spiritual health.

He deals well with what it means for us to be filled with the Holy Spirit. This might be new to some or take them out of their comfort zone, but Alister's gentle and instructive sensitivity eases any anxiety that there may be for those who desire to encounter the Spirit through dreams, prayer or prophecy.

In his desire to explain the Biblical basis for his transformation, there are passages of theology which need careful attention in order for the reader to deepen their relationship with Jesus. As a church leader, I found myself highlighting parts which would be ideal for preaching and teaching purposes. The descriptions and explanations of some profound theological terms (covenant, circumcision, Fatherhood of God, etc.) are spot on, and Alister succeeds in debunking some Christianese terms! His teaching is accessible to everyone – people of faith or none.

The final section gives the reader an opportunity to engage in Bible study and self-reflection. Be prepared to be challenged. The questions may elicit strong feelings, trauma or pain, so I encourage the reader to work alongside a trusted friend, mentor or prayer partner.

Alister's love for Jesus, his wife Lesley, his family and the church is palpable. He shows great vulnerability and honesty. That is rare in some Christian circles and it is a breath of fresh air. His openness to the Holy Spirit, particularly in dreams and prophecy, is really encouraging, and challenged me to be more open to praying in the Spirit.

This book is an intelligent, articulate insight into the heart of what it means to follow Jesus and seek Him in every circumstance. It is a genuine, honest cry of a broken man to a loving Heavenly Father who brings healing, restoration and the desire for more of the Holy Spirit. I would recommend this book to pastors, teachers and leaders who wish to take their people into a deeper relationship with Father God. There is a wealth of knowledge which will be useful for small groups or reading groups for discussion. Ministry and prayer teams will benefit from the teaching on prophecy and healing. Anyone with anxiety, depression or other mental health issues will find this book an effective tool to face those demons and overcome by the power of the Spirit. It inspires confidence in God to free us from our religiosity into a deeper relationship with Father, Son and Holy Spirit.

Reverend Irene Campbell
Family and Community Pastor
Westwood Baptist Church, East Kilbride

Introduction

The impetus for writing this book was rather unexpected and happened in a local hotel over a civilised cup of coffee. I was with a friend, James, half way through a conversation about some innocuous subject – my family? the latest movies? the nature of faith in God? the decline of high street shopping? – when James suddenly skewered me with a blunt suggestion: 'You should write a book!' I stopped blathering for a moment and held my cup of coffee in an awkward pose, as I sought to comprehend the curt instruction and the strange workings of my friend's mind. However, his pitch to write a book – or was it a command? – struck a deep chord within me, as the thought of a book had long been stirring up inside me. This interjection over coffee proved to be the firing of a starting gun for what you have in front of you.

Three or four months after the starting gun was fired, I lifted my feet off the blocks and started writing. (The gap between hearing the gun and springing into action is embarrassing evidence of a delayed reaction – the story of my life!) I knew that the subject matter of the book was going to be my long and difficult battle with mental health problems – specifically, acute anxiety and depression. It was also going to be about my faith in, and extraordinary experiences of, a loving God who took me from a very low place of suicidal thoughts and feelings, to an elevated one of renewed hope and inner drive. The recovery process is far from over, however, and I remain to this day in a state of partial brokenness – hence the book's title.

Reflections of a Broken Son

On the morning that I sat down to begin writing, furnished with nothing more than a book title, I prayed to Father God for a roadmap to follow. Almost immediately, the chapter headings of the book came to my mind in a hot lava stream of ideas that spilled out onto a blank spreadsheet. (I have been a researcher for more than half of my life, so spreadsheets are some of my best friends.) Armed with chapter headings and bullet points under each heading, I ventured forth into the great unknown. I knew one thing at the offset: I was not going to be po-faced about a difficult subject, nor superficial for that matter. I hope that I have ended up striking a balanced tone. You, dear reader, will be the ultimate judge of that.

This is the journey of a splintered man graciously touched by a compassionate God who delights in restoring the broken-hearted. God is my witness that all of the events depicted in this book happened as described.

Alister

Chapter 1

Humpty Dumpty

In 1986, I lay alone in a bed in my girlfriend's work flat one Sunday morning in Greenock, a 27-year old man broken on the inside. Distraught and deeply afraid, I was drowning in a pool of suicidal thoughts. Painful emotions, normally kept hidden from view, now forced their way out into the open. I wept in the privacy of the empty room, unleashing an anguished cry up to heaven, hoping that God was at home and able to throw me a lifeline. I opened my mouth to pray and words came tumbling out, raw and heartfelt. (If you want to know what an honest prayer sounds like, listen to the plaintive cry of someone trapped in an infernal place with no obvious means of escape. I have no doubts at all that Jonah, Old Testament prophet and one-time occupant of a whale's belly, discovered an honest way to pray in the time of his own hellish confinement.)

Opening my mouth in that small unadorned bedroom over thirty years ago, words punctuated by sobs ascended to heaven, a river of self-pity directed upwards. What I remember praying out loud, as I stared up at the ceiling, was heartsick and close to this:

> *God, if you're up there, please help me. I've made a total mess of everything. I'm an idiot and*

Reflections of a Broken Son

I've fallen off a wall. I'm all humpty dumpty down here, broken to bits, and I don't have the strength to get back up off the ground. Please put my life back together again. Rebuild me, please!

Now before you think that I was a religious devotee offering up a pious prayer to God, nothing could be further from the truth. Instead, I was a postgraduate student that year and a dedicated drunk: *functional alcoholic* is the certified term. The twin sponsors of my drinking habit were self-doubt and discontentment. So, my prayer that morning was far from religious devotion; it was the release of a gut-wrenching cry from within, an unvarnished plea for divine intervention.

Lying in my misery, I suddenly became aware of a heightened feeling inside me, a sense of urgency and prompting. An insistent thought pushed its way into my consciousness: *Go to church today!* The thought felt distinct from my own thoughts, firmly cutting through them, and not an instruction that I would have readily spoken over myself. I did not fully realise at the time that this was the voice of my heavenly Father seeking to pull me up out of my self-made swamp, not yet being familiar with his affectionate tones and fatherly ways, I only knew that I had definitely heard something in my heart, pressing and persuasive. The idea of stepping into a church building to seek help, however, did not sit well with me, to say the least. So began a fierce tug of war inside me for the main part of that day.

When I eventually conceded to the mysterious directive to go to church, more out of emotional fatigue than happy compliance, I headed off to a place of worship that evening like a sullen child dragging his heels all the way to school. Standing outside the doors of a church in Glasgow, I suddenly had a moment of panic. My internal tug of war had now reached a dizzy climax, with one inner voice calmly urging me to go inside and another hollering at me to run away for dear life. (Picture *Oor Wullie,* a famous Scottish fictional character, with a sweet-talking angel on one shoulder and a pitchfork-wielding demon on the other.) For the next twenty minutes, I paced back and forth between the entrance to the church and the traffic lights a short distance away, with a view to crossing the road and retreating back to my personal hell. I must have looked ill, peculiar or both. In the end, however, my fear of returning to a world of pain was ultimately outweighed by self-preservation and a burning curiosity to find out why I had to go to church that day.

Inside the church, an assembly of mostly young people, many of them university students like myself, had gathered, awaiting the start of the service. I sat with my head bowed low at the back of the congregation, feeling socially inept and hoping that my secret power of anonymity would hold out. However, God had a different plan for me that evening, sending someone to disturb my solitude. An obstinately cheerful Christian, whose name I have since forgotten but whose sunny deportment I remember well, sat beside me with a broad smile on his face. For an uncomfortable while he peppered me with some upbeat courtesies, which my dead heart was incapable of returning.

My newfound companion quickly cut off his brave attempts to connect with me as the church band mercifully struck up a tune. The meeting had begun. I listened, pleasantly surprised at the contemporary sounds and absorbing the non-stuffy atmosphere without directly engaging with it, being unfamiliar with the reverential words and pop-sounding tunes. It was just a relief to switch off my troubled mind for a short while and not have to think.

At the end of the worship, the pastor of the church stood up to speak. He was an older man with a relaxed manner. He began by declaring that he had 'words of knowledge' from God for three different people. Although I had never heard this expression before, I reasoned that the pastor was claiming that God had given him important messages for people in his congregation. (I later discovered reference to words of knowledge in the Bible, where the word of knowledge is described as a manifestation of the Holy Spirit given for a good and helpful purpose (see 1 Cor. 12:7-11). Essentially, it is a personal word from the heart of God, mediated through believers in Christ, for the benefit of an intended hearer.)

By now, I was sitting bolt upright in my seat, my hang-dog demeanour temporarily suspended. This was refreshingly new to me, and I braced myself in hope of a sign from heaven; anything to resolve my interior pain. However, the first word spoken by the pastor came and went like a damp squib, a huge disappointment to me but no doubt of great significance and comfort to someone else. Then, just prior to the pastor delivering his second word, an unexpected cloud of heat burst over me, a strange and intense tingling sensation that covered the surface of my body. In my heart, I once again heard the still, small voice that I had heard that morning: *Listen carefully, the next word is for you!*

The next word to come out of the pastor's mouth was to alter my life permanently, striking me like a bolt of lightning from heaven. In that moment, these extraordinary words – extraordinary to me at any rate – came out of a man's mouth:

> *Somebody here tonight put up an urgent prayer to God this morning. He has heard your cry for help and has this to say to you: 'I will restore you.'*

At this point, I almost leapt off of my chair with excitement. I did not, and could not, take anything else on board after that utterance; it was a glorious shaft of light in my darkness and a stunning promise. My mind was frantically racing. Several thoughts crowded in at once, most prominent being an awareness that God appeared to be alive, capable of communicating and, more to the point, offering to restore my life as I had urgently petitioned him that morning. He had spoken directly to my own heart and was now unmistakably

Humpty Dumpty

speaking to me through another person. It was revelatory; even downright revolutionary. After all, wasn't God supposed to be dead? Was he not merely the fictional product of needy people clinging to rumours of heaven? Or the idle muse of religious conscripts and bores? That's what my former closed mindset had taught me. My head was now buzzing with the implications of a God who spoke in a personal way.

After the service had ended, I accosted the pastor and subjected him to a wind tunnel of fervent gratitude for his second word of knowledge delivered from the pulpit (a lectern, to be precise). With contrasting restraint, he requested politely that I remind him exactly of which word I was referring to. (This was my first church-based lesson in realising that the world did not spin on its axis around me.) When I breathlessly recounted to him what he had said, he smiled and shook my hand like a statesman, wishing me well. (We later became friends and cool courtesy was replaced with warm affection and pastoral care.) I got the feeling that I had just made a fool of myself but, in the joy of that moment, I was too enthralled by the fact that God was alive and had promised to put this humpty dumpty back together again. What I did not realise, back then, was that my journey into personal restoration would not be automatic: divine help would be close at hand and freely available, but it would also require freewill responses on my part to God's loving counsel and restorative touch.

The trajectory of my life flowing out of God's initial promise to restore me is what this book is all about. It is my first-hand account of a God who cares, even when it seems like he doesn't, offering hope to those who are disenchanted with religion, in a world often torn apart by it. It is also written to encourage those who may secretly wonder if God can really deal with their emotional pain. But before I describe my step-wise journey into personal restoration by a loving Father – specifically the God of the Bible and the Father of Jesus Christ, his Son – I need to

Reflections of a Broken Son

reveal how I got to the point of harbouring suicidal thoughts. I need to explain the events that led to me crying helplessly in a bed in Greenock in the mid-1980s, bringing me to a sore and difficult place of calling out to heaven for help.

Chapter 2

Freefalling

I gained admission to university in 1977. I was 18-years old and the future, with all its brilliant possibilities, stretched out in front of me. The heady whirl of fresh experiences and a bourgeoning social life were the highpoints of student life. Over the first four years, I enjoyed frequenting the various bars in and around campus, striking up new friendships and drinking happily in the afternoons and evenings. Throughout this period, my alcohol intake was not excessive, but the seeds of problem drinking were being steadily sown in my life. I was inching my way on a downward slope to a dark emotional place.

It was around fifth year at university that alcohol as a tool to lift my mood morphed into a propensity to self-medicate. This included repeatedly attending lectures with alcohol in my system, not enough to draw attention to myself but sufficient to grant me courage to be around people and speak in public. On one occasion, I overstepped the mark, slurring my way through a class presentation and bringing a look of horror to the face of the lecturer. Oblivious to my growing dilemma, alcohol was gaining a foothold in my life, progressively warping my outlook and personality. That I went on to gain a first-class honours degree that year was a minor academic miracle, but my increasingly troubled relationship with alcohol did not stop me from studying hard. I could still step up to the mark and deliver when required.

In point of view, there is no stereotypical functional alcoholic: we blend in like social chameleons, expertly masking our problems. As for my own problems, I possessed an anxious disposition, later to surface uncontrollably, that fuelled and aggravated my drinking behaviour. The drinking subsequently fed back into my anxieties, amplifying them, requiring further use of alcohol to subdue my fears. It was a vicious cycle, ruthlessly beating down my self-confidence. By now, the effort to quell my fears was beginning to exact a hefty toll on me.

Other parallel forces were at play in my life at that time that began to slip under the gravitational pull of my drinking problems. Back in 1977, as a new student, I had embarked on a quest for existential meaning and purpose, driven by simple curiosity. Five years later, as I dropped down an emotional sinkhole, this straightforward quest became more of an expedition to find my way out of pain. Seeking freedom, I explored Buddhism and Taoism, and devoured an impressive array of self-help literature. On the other hand, the three major monotheistic faiths of Islam, Judaism and Christianity were off-limits to me because I saw them as fast tracks to restriction rather than release. Despite this resistance, I eventually picked up the Bible, but a cursory plunge into the Old Testament left me with a slanted view of God as a cruel and vengeful deity. This early venture into the Scriptures left me with a bad taste in my mouth, pushing God out to the margins of my quest for truth.

As my continued search for peace proved fruitless, however, I found myself giving Christianity another chance, this time approaching the Scriptures through the New Testament. I knew a few Christians at university and one of them had dropped a small pocket-sized edition of John's Gospel into my hand. Savouring John's distinctive account of Jesus, my defences against Christianity gradually began to lower. Unlike the other gospel writers – Matthew, Mark and Luke – John cast a steady spotlight on the character of Jesus, stressing his identity and portraying his miracles as indicators of higher truths about the nature and purposes of God. John was a connoisseur of the meaning of Jesus' words and actions. As a first-hand witness of events, his account is marked by intimacy, reflecting the insights of a man who had often reclined his head on Jesus' chest, listening attentively to his extraordinary words. His gospel is a symphony of love to the Son and his eternal Father, and it had begun to dig its way secretly into my heart.

One night in my bedroom, while I was still living at home with my family, I had reached a critical point in my emerging faith through closely studying John's Gospel. (Without realising it at the time, I was exemplifying the Apostle Paul's assertion in Romans 10:17 that faith arises on account of hearing the good news about Christ.) The claims of Jesus about himself were bubbling in my thoughts. Among his many bold claims, the seven great *I am* declarations stood tall in my mind that night: *"I am the bread of life"* (John 6:35); *"I am the light of the world"* (John 8:12); *"I am the gate"* (John 10:9); *"I am the good shepherd"* (John 10:11); *"I am the resurrection and the life"* (John 11:25); *"I am the way, the truth and the life"* (John 14:6); and *"I am the vine"* (John 15:5). It appeared to me that everything Jesus ever said about himself crackled with life and authenticity. I had come to believe that he was the one whom he claimed to be, and now I was ready to open up my heart to him.

Alone in the half-light of my bedroom – my brother with whom I shared the room had gone out that night socialising with friends – I opened my mouth and let words and tears fly. To help me pray for the first time in my adult life, I formed a picture in my head of Jesus standing at the right-hand side of his Father in heaven, with his arms stretched out in compassion. With this helpful image to support me, I released my pain up to Jesus, asking him repeatedly for forgiveness. For a while, I let my anguished thoughts and emotions pour out uninhibitedly to

Reflections of a Broken Son

Jesus. At a certain point, I stopped and trailed off mid-sentence: the room suddenly felt on fire. The heat was intense, and I can only describe it as pins and needles flickering and dancing all over my body. (I would experience this unusual phenomenon one more time, four years later in a church, as described in the first chapter.) Though my whole body was affected, the heat was concentrated around my hands and mouth. While I found the physical sensations uncomfortable, I quickly shifted into a settled feeling of calmness and let the experience run its course. Lying still in bed, I remained silent, unable to process what had just happened.

The next day, in between lectures, I collared a Christian whom I knew at that time. With some trepidation, I told him about the unusual events of the previous evening. He stared at me quizzically, more a look of bewilderment than disapproval. Neither dismissing nor validating my story, he simply said that it lay outside the scope of his own understanding and experience. Though gracious in his response to me, I was quietly devastated at the lack of unequivocal affirmation. Something within me died in that moment, and I stepped away from God back into the illusory safety of my ignorance, privately vowing not to speak again about my experience. (I would only open up to a select few people over subsequent years, until I became more assured of myself and what had happened to me in my bedroom.)

Having shut down my heart to God, the next four years of my life were incredibly difficult. My drinking problems spiralled as I began to drink in the morning and behind the backs of family and friends, all of the while maintaining a composed but increasingly fragile front. Feelings of inadequacy and low self-worth ruled my inner world, defiling everything that I experienced including relationships, and each day was a painful exercise in camouflaging my insecurities. The pain even felt physical, as if a heavy bowling ball of dread had taken up residency in my chest. I was becoming ill and felt hopelessly lost in my emotional wilderness.

This internal pressure was bound to reach critical mass eventually. When it finally did, the crescendo came as more of an implosion than an explosion. I was with my girlfriend at a gathering of her relatives in the suburbs of Glasgow. Enjoying the drinks and snacks on offer, I sat down to talk with a cousin of my girlfriend. Although I had been feeling self-conscious, I was in a friendly environment and in fine conversational flow. Without warning, a paralysing fear suddenly overtook me: I was experiencing the mother of panic attacks. My vision went strangely dark and my stomach lurched. The people in the room appeared as shadows and silhouettes to me, as fear seemed to fill every nook and cranny of my being, even to the clouding of my vision. I could hear my name being called out, as if from a distance, but I was unable to pull myself quickly out of the hellish quicksand that had ambushed me. It took a few excruciating moments to recover. Recomposing myself, I shied away from offering an explanation for my shutdown, more out of embarrassment than anything else.

This avoidance of disclosing my problems became an ingrained feature of my life over a considerable period of time. Soldiering on, it would take another twenty years before I would be issued with a formal diagnosis of anxiety and depression. (One clinician would even describe the worst symptoms of my condition as being akin to trauma.) Throughout this lengthy period of time, the damage that I ended up inflicting on myself by not dealing with my problems was enormous. My reticence to deal with them meant that a claw of persistent anxiety was given scope to burrow down into a very deep place within me. (I use this metaphor deliberately and will revisit this image later in the book.)

In many ways, I felt like two different people back then. The person I projected in public could be gregarious, laugh and joke, and live quite normally, at least in outward terms. Meanwhile, the person I hid from view was crippled by anxiety and prone to flight when things got tough, relationally or otherwise. Under the surface, in my secluded combat zone, I was warring with an army of hostile, self-defeating thoughts and feelings. Some days, I felt like a lodging house for every human insecurity that ever existed. It was into this cesspool of low self-esteem that thoughts of suicide stole their way into my mind. At 27-years old, four years after turning my back on God, I was finally running out of road and the strength to go on.

What I did not take into account, however, was a heavenly Father relentless in his love for his children (1 John 4:7-12). He was not about to abandon me, having already reached out to me. With compassion, the Father broke into my heart one night with a remarkable and highly vivid dream of his Son, Jesus, on the cross. In the dream, I saw myself delivered from a place of great distress to one of safety. (I will explore the finer details of the dream in chapter 5.) It was a heaven-sent message of hope showing me a clear path out of my torment and confinement. The dream firmly placed Jesus back to the front of my consciousness, reminding me that I had once looked to him for help only to retreat hastily in ignorance. God's persistence was proving stronger than my pig-headedness.

It was a short while following this dream that I would be lying in another bed in Greenock and praying for my life to be put back together, in turn to receive a personal promise of restoration from God. I came to understand later that the dream of the cross was evidence of the Holy Spirit secretly at work in my heart, paving the way for me to be reconciled back to my loving Father by the only route open to us all: the blood of Jesus Christ (Col. 1:19-20). By dying in our place, the Son has extended to us the gracious and unparalleled promise of being reconciled to the Father (Rom. 5:10). In turn, we are able to lay hold of this wonderful gift from heaven by means of faith (Acts 16:31).

Freefalling

The Father's promise to restore me had now put my feet on the rock-solid ground of his love, which was to set me off in a new life-affirming direction. Further revelations and encouraging touches from him were to follow, but not without some serious bumps in the road. I was soon to discover that a broken heart does not fix so easily.

Reflections of a Broken Son

Chapter 3

The Big Picture

When I was a child, I walked a line between extroversion and introversion. In my more extroverted mode, I would hang out with a group of friends every summer, frequently tearing through people's back gardens in the estate where I lived. We would race like hurdlers, propelled by adrenaline and the prospect of red-faced neighbours hammering on their windows as we hid behind their bushes or, sometimes, just hurtled past like a pack of delinquent express trains. On one occasion, somewhat in the manner of a Tex Avery cartoon, a friend of my brother ran in a blind panic into a tall creosoted fence as an inhabitant of one house suddenly appeared at the window. Rumour had it that the particular residents of the house in question were members of a famous pop group in the 1970s. This piece of pop trivia, true or otherwise, was of no help to my brother's friend at the time of his concussion, though he recovered quickly.

In my less interesting though decidedly safer introverted mode, I had a passion for jigsaw puzzles, as well as for building bricks and construction models; basically, any toy that involved assembling parts. I loved the challenge of seeing the picture on the front of a jigsaw box and recreating that image. Still life pictures did not hold my interest: pictures of busy market places in exotic locations was more my scene in the fast lane of the jigsaw-puzzling world. Having sight of the picture helped settle my choice to invest time in completing a jigsaw. The box-cover picture was also a roadmap, a friendly guide to assist the construction process.

Looking back, I realise that my spiritual journey did not have a clear focus at the start, as I stumbled from one experience and revelation to another with no clear sight of where I was headed. The problem was not lack of a reliable roadmap to hand: the potent combination of God's word (2 Tim. 3:16-17) and the indwelling Spirit of God (John 14:16-17) is all the roadmap that we will ever need in this earthly life. On the contrary, the problem in the early part of my walk with God was a combination of possessing a stubborn heart and of being saddled with a deep bedrock of pain in my soul. I can see now that my troubles, at that time, were powered by a pervasive sense of shame and fear. Though largely unaware of the big picture at the start, I am grateful to the Father for his unrivalled patience, working tirelessly over a long period of time to soften my heart and illuminate my mind. The Apostle Paul expressed his own appreciation of God's patience in this way:

> *Here is a trustworthy saying that deserves full acceptance: Christ Jesus came into the world to save sinners – of whom I am the worst. But for that very reason I was shown mercy so that in me, the worst of sinners, Christ Jesus might display his immense patience as an example for those who would believe in him and receive eternal life.*
>
> 1 Tim. 1:15-16, NIVUK

As I prepare to detail the outworking of God's patience in my own life in the chapters ahead, I will take opportunity here, in the remaining part of this chapter, to provide context and set out a fundamental roadmap of divine restoration. To do this, a

The Big Picture

spotlight will be cast on events that took place when humanity fell in the Garden of Eden. The story of the Fall is found in chapter 3 of the Book of Genesis. Through this story, we can gain an understanding of the origin of sin and our subsequent estrangement from Father God, but also glean insight into the Father's unwavering determination to restore us back to intimacy with him.

....

Essentially, the fall of the human race unfolded like this:

Dwelling in an idyllic garden and secure within the provisions of a fiercely loving God, our original human parents, Adam and Eve, wanted for nothing. Intimacy between God and his beloved children – those whom he had fashioned by his own hand and in his own image – was undisturbed. Two beautiful trees stood at the centre of the garden: the Tree of Life and the Tree of the Knowledge of Good and Evil. The fruit of the former bestowed immortality, while that of the latter had the capacity to open a person's eyes to see good and evil like God. Though Adam and Eve were granted all-areas access within their lush paradise, the Father warned them not to eat from the Tree of Knowledge, telling them in clear terms that if they defied this instruction then they would certainly die.

Enter the defiler of innocence: Satan, in the guise of a commonplace serpent. Infuriated by the sight of intimacy between the heavenly Father and his children, a privilege he himself had once enjoyed before his mutinous actions got him cast out of heaven, the serpent began plotting revenge. (The full account of Satan's fall can be found in Ezekiel 28 and Isaiah 14.) With cold resolve and an orphaned heart, the serpent set his sights on ruining paradise. In his irredeemable alienation, his only instinct was to replicate in others his own distorted image.

Reflections of a Broken Son

One day, he saw his chance and sneaked up on the woman. Now, the serpent was above all things cunning, and feigned to play the honest broker. With condescending genius, he questioned God's goodness towards Eve by directing her attention to the only embargo that God had laid down in Eden: not to eat fruit from the Tree of Knowledge. The serpent put it to Eve that the Lord God was withholding something of great value from her. Challenging God's express command, Satan tempted Eve to relinquish her trust in God and eat the forbidden fruit. The serpent spoke of her eyes being opened and of being able to distinguish good and evil for herself, thereby releasing her to live by her own wits.

Beneath the sales pitch, Satan was hard at work to lure Eve into a trap of estrangement from her doting Father. Like all con artists, he failed to mention the catch buried in the small print. For lurking within his proposition to defy God's command lay a tripwire, ready to set off a charge in the hearts of Adam and Eve that would hurl them into a tailspin of bad decisions and fractured relationships. Sadly, the allure of possessing a self-governing wisdom was too much to resist for our original parents. Falling for Satan's ploy, they ate the prohibited fruit and succumbed to the oldest temptation of all: to make ourselves like the Most High (Isa. 14:14). This was the great conceit that lay at the heart of the Fall, corrupting everything it touched. A sense of orphanness had now stolen its way into the human heart, secreted in by the king orphan himself.

If that was where the story had ended, then the human race would have pretty much ended there too, or shortly thereafter. Thankfully, having already judged all that he had created to be *very good* (Gen. 1:31), God was not about to develop a streak of indifference and abandon his prized creations. An undimmed and iridescent love was ablaze in the heart of the Father towards his children, and he already knew what he had to do to rescue his wayward offspring.

The Big Picture

Meanwhile, with eyes opened from eating fruit from the Tree of Knowledge, innocence had slipped away from Adam and Eve and they became self-consciously aware of their nakedness. Now, recast in the garden as self-directing entities, they felt ashamed and frightened, alone with no clear way out of their predicament. Intimacy with God, once their rightful inheritance, had been stolen from under their noses. Adrift from that safeguarding intimacy, they sought to deal with their problems through the soon-to-be established pattern of masking them and hiding themselves away – in this instance, using fig leaves and trees for cover – actions that would prove worthless and only serve to make a bad situation worse.

Enter the restorer of innocence: the Lord God, walking in the garden in the cool of the day. Driven by a selfless love burning in his heart, God called Adam and Eve out from their hiding places in the trees. Reluctantly, they stood before their God. The Lord God spelled out the consequences of their disobedience: pain of childbirth for Eve; the curse of hard labour and sweat for Adam; and pronouncement of judgment on the serpent that he would be crushed in future by the woman's seed (a descendant born through her line). Within this last penalty was a glorious promise to humanity: God's gift of salvation. The seed of the woman would eventually take the form of the Father's Son, Jesus Christ, sent to bear our sins and restore us back to the Father's loving presence. The Son would break the oppressive reign of the king orphan over humanity, because, in his devotion to his children, the eternal Father could not bear to leave them as orphans in this world. (Jesus would later confirm and authorise this very promise to his disciples before heading to the cross; see John 14:18.)

In acts of consummate kindness, God clothed Adam and Eve with the skins of animals to cover their nakedness, then sent them away from the Garden of Eden, preventing them from eating fruit from the Tree of Life and thereby rescuing them from an endless abysmal internment of fallenness. For the Father was looking out for his children, the only thing that his tender heart was capable of doing. Paradise may have been momentarily lost, but God was busy securing a confident future for the human race and raising a banner of lasting hope, later to be revealed and fulfilled in his Son. Divine love would win the day, and what was once lost would be restored.

....

The above outline of the Fall and the Restoration provides a backdrop to the rest of this book. In the chapters that follow, my own personal journey from spiritual orphanness to sonship is described. The term *sonship* should not be understood here as being the province of males, for there is strictly no hierarchy of male and female in Christ (Gal. 3:28). It should be understood as an indiscriminate term, encompassing people of every gender, race and social status, and signifying our gracious standing in the Father as his beloved children, through faith in Christ. In addition, the term *orphanness* should be understood as a spiritual state, the condition of a human heart distanced from, or out of alignment with, the love of the Father. This is not unique to the unsaved heart; it also applies to Christians, even Spirit-filled ones, who still bear traits of orphanness, a legacy of the Fall, in areas of their lives yet unsurrendered to the Father's love. (I will be sure to divulge some of my own shortcomings, in this respect, by way of illustration.) The deeper meanings of sonship and orphanness will unfold in the chapters ahead.

Before describing my journey into the depths of sonship, however, I am particularly keen to stress pursuit of the Father over and above what he can do for us. Experiences are important, but the primary purpose in life should always be to

The Big Picture

press into deeper intimacy with the Father. I use specific experiences herein only to illustrate the imprint of God's grace (his unearned favour) upon a human life, and the impact of his patient care in restoring a broken man back to authentic sonship. Each person, like every character in the Bible, requires his or her own unique relationship with God (Eph. 1:4-6), together with an adventure of faith marked by inimitable experiences (see Hebrews 11). And with the hearts of restored children, as opposed to that of spiritual orphans, we can rejoice in each other's adventure without looking enviously or disapprovingly across the way. Let the journey begin.

Reflections of a Broken Son

Chapter 4

The Father's Promise

Every journey has a beginning. My own spiritual journey took off decisively at the point when I received a direct promise from Father God of restoration. Deeper into this journey, I now realise that this personal promise sits within, and has only been made possible by, a wider promise given by God to Abraham. This wider promise is known as the Abrahamic promise. I will use the terms *Abrahamic promise* and *Father's promise* interchangeably in this chapter to signify this particular promise.

To better understand how God is able to restore people's lives, it is necessary to appreciate the nature of the Abrahamic promise, which is the solid foundation undergirding and safeguarding our journey into divine restoration. Like a fog slowly lifting, I have come to realise that the Father's promise has always been the key to that journey. I have further come to accept as true that the private promise given to me (*'I will restore you'*) was simply a targeted offshoot of the more encompassing promise made to Abraham, itself foreshadowed by a divine promise first decreed in the Garden of Eden.

Now, there are at least five key elements to any promise given from one person to another:

- *From whom* — the person making the promise
- *To whom* — the beneficiary of the promise
- *What is given* — the nature of the promise itself
- *How given* — how the promise is issued
- *How received* — how the promise is appropriated.

Examination of each of these five key elements follows, and will cast light on God as an eternally loving Father who delights in his children, devoted to fortifying their lives with comforting certainties rather than uneasy vagaries.

From Whom: The Trustworthy Father

Ask ten different people to tell you what someone is like and you will likely get ten distinct, and sometimes even contrary, opinions. Behold the enigma of the individual: the supportive friend and annoying work colleague; the witty raconteur and interminable bore; the self-sacrificing parent and self-absorbed egotist. One person can appear many different ways to different observers, depending on what witnesses draw out of a person in their unique encounters with them, and on what perspective, critical or charitable, they bring to bear on their scrutiny of a person. As someone who has suffered a great deal in his adult life from social anxiety, I have found myself, in moments of intense shyness, being subject to cutting remarks of 'bore' and 'socially awkward'. On other occasions, when I have been able to push past the cactus spines of my self-protection, allowing the soft internal tissue of a warm personality to pop into view, I have made staunch friends who have prized my company. It would seem, then, that we live in a world surrounded by people on a spectrum from sniping critic to loyal supporter. This is the conflicting reality running through many, if not all, people's lives.

The Father's Promise

The same inconsistencies apply when asking people to express their opinions about God. To some, he is the absent landlord presiding over his rented-out universe, leaving the tenants to pretty much fend for themselves. To others, he is the celestial police officer parked in the lay-bys of our lives with a handheld speed camera. To the children of his promise, however, he is the generous, open-hearted dreamer who envisioned a way for wayward souls to return to him, and then made it all possible through his beloved Son, Jesus Christ. And to the heirs of his kingdom, he is the perpetual giver lavishing his children with fatherly affections and gifts.

To navigate through the choppy waters of these contradictions, we need a reliable chart to guide us. For such a purpose, the Father has given us his living word, sharp and able to cut through our intellectual and attitudinal barricades (Heb. 4:12). In view of this, and regarding what the Scriptures have to say about the character of God, there is one attribute of the Father that stands out and by which all of his other attributes can be framed: love. The Apostle John recognised this pivotal attribute, clearly reflected in the Son who is the express image of his Father (Heb. 1:3), proclaiming assuredly that God is love (1 John 4:8,16). Love is essentially the default position of the Father's heart. While he undeniably hates sin and the indignities that people inflict on each other (Ps. 5:4; Zech. 8:17), he is nonetheless disposed to love us (John 3:16; Rom. 5:8), seeking to draw us back to himself through his Son (John 6:44). This is not an argument for the automatic salvation of people, but rather an argument for the perennial love abiding in the heart of the Father.

Once we recognise the reality of the Father's love, the case for his trustworthiness virtually becomes a given. Still, let us pose the blunt question at any rate: can God be trusted? The Bible is unequivocal about this matter: first, God is utterly faithful and dependable (Isa. 25:1; Lam. 3:22-23); second, as a consummate truth-teller, he is incapable of lying (Ps. 119:160; Rom. 3:3-4);

and third, he calls those who walk in his ways also to uphold the truth (Eph. 6:14; 2 Tim. 2:15), hardly the expression of an untrustworthy character. In short, trustworthiness courses through every strand of God's being, pervading every inch of his spiritual DNA. He is the resolute Father, unwavering in his faithfulness, and this is the unshakeable foundation upon which we can put our trust in him, both as our promise-giver and promise-keeper.

To Whom: All Peoples on Earth

The true scope of the Father's promise and its beneficiaries is clearly laid out in God's declaration to Abraham:

> *I will make you into a great nation,*
>   *and I will bless you;*
> *I will make your name great,*
>   *and you will be a blessing.*
> *I will bless those who bless you,*
>   *and whoever curses you I will curse;*
> *and all peoples on earth*
>   *will be blessed through you.*
>
> Gen 12:2-3, NIVUK

Thus, when God promised to bless Abraham, he cast a keen fatherly eye beyond Abraham, setting in motion a river of blessing, rippling out from heaven to reach all peoples on earth. In truth, he is not the God of half measures or modest exertions, especially when it comes to seeking out and rescuing the lost souls of this world (Ezek. 34:11-16; Matt. 18:12-14). His reach is energetic and all-inclusive, with the whole earth serving as his searching ground (Zech. 4:10; Ps. 102:19). Moreover, the Son who takes after his heavenly Father (John 5:19), is likewise expansive in his purpose, holding out his generous offer of salvation to the entire world (John 1:29; 1 John 4:14). All peoples on earth are invited to enter God's kingdom without exception (Matt. 28:19-20), and no-one who draws near to God will ever be turned away by him (John 7:37; James 4:8). The problem is therefore one of self-exclusion, realised through hardness of heart towards God (Matt. 13:15; Rom. 2:5). Even so, God is willing that none should perish (2 Pet. 3:9), and his promise of blessing pours down from heaven upon all peoples of all nations, without partiality or discrimination (Acts 10:34).

What is Given: The Promise of Restored Lives

Within the Abrahamic promise, God made three distinct and unified promises to Abraham: these are the promises of blessing, descendants and land. An account of these three intertwined promises is found in Genesis 12, 15 and 17. As stated before, the promise of blessing was not exclusive to Abraham. It is a torrent of blessing raining down from heaven in pursuit of hearts open to God in the manner of Abraham's heart (Rom. 4:11-12). How this heavenly flow of blessing relates to our lives today is detailed by the Apostle Paul in Galatians 3:1-4:7. In this key passage, Paul describes the promise of blessing from a New Testament perspective, splitting it into three interconnected parts: the promise of the Holy Spirit (Gal. 3:1-14); the promise of salvation through *the seed,* Jesus Christ (Gal. 3:15-22); and the promise of sonship to the Father (Gal. 3:23-4:7). Examining each of these New Testament promises, will show that each is an integral part of God's plan to restore our lives back to the uninterrupted intimacy that we enjoyed with the Father before the Fall. As the gateway into this blessing, salvation through Christ is explored first.

The promise of salvation through Jesus Christ: In the previous chapter of this book, we noted that God issued a promise in the Garden of Eden, announcing that a seed (descendant) would come in due time through the woman, crushing the serpent's head and saving humanity (Gen. 3:15).

This is the Edenic promise, foretelling the recovery of fallen lives through intervention of an exceptional seed (singular). A link is established between the Edenic and Abrahamic promises when Paul notes that the latter was given to Abraham and his seed (again singular). Paul then asserts that the promised seed is none other than Christ (Gal. 3:16). It is clear, therefore, that the seeds alluded to in both promises are one and the same person: Jesus Christ. This is the Son whom the Father sent from heaven to save us (John 3:16-17), dying in our place to grant us peace with God (Rom. 5:1), securing our adoption as children to the heavenly Father (Eph. 1:4-5), and granting us an inheritance along with himself as co-heir (Rom. 8:17).

In short, the Son is the living pathway to restoration, guiding us back into relationship with the Father (2 Cor. 5:18-20).

The promise of the Holy Spirit: Paul addresses the promise of the Spirit in the context of a serious problem that had arisen in the church of Galatia. Due to the intrusions and meddling of false teachers, the Galatian believers had veered away from the straightforward message of salvation through faith in Christ and were regressing to patterns of ritualistic and rule-based behaviour (*works of the law*) (Gal. 3:1-2). Paul reminded them that the miracles that the Spirit had performed among them at the start of their Christian experience, had been released on account of their simple faith in the message of Christ and not according to their own pious efforts (Gal. 3:5). He then urged them to get back to their uncomplicated faith in the Gospel and embrace the promise of the Spirit (Gal. 3:14). Elsewhere in his writings, Paul urges believers to be filled with the Spirit (Eph. 5:18). This is the Spirit who dwells in our physical bodies (1 Cor. 6:19), imprinting the Father's ways onto our hearts (Ezek. 36:27), renewing us to Christ-likeness (Gal. 5:22-23), and empowering us to live in newness of life (Rom. 8:11).

The Father's Promise

In short, the Spirit is the enabler of restoration, driving our lives deeper into the Father's loving ways and confirming that we are his children (Rom. 8:14).

The promise of sonship to the Father: As sons and daughters of the Father, we are marked out as such through our faith in Christ and not through rule-based behaviour (Gal. 3:23-25). We are to trust in the Father's good intentions towards us and in his ability to restore our lives, not in our own imperfect labours and self-improvements. We do not *do* works of any sort to become the Father's children: we *are* his children by virtue of his loving initiative (1 John 4:10) and an inward and supernatural rebirthing (John 1:12-13). As true children, we act out of our Father's love, and not according to some dutiful impulse to please him. The Father puts the Spirit of sonship into our hearts and a joyous cry rises up from within us in recognition that we belong to the Father (Gal. 4:6). We do not have to try to be his kids any more than our own earthly children have to try to be ours. Inherently, we are his children and he loves us; purely and simply. This is the Father who chose us before creation (Eph. 1:11), declares us to be his treasured possession (Exo. 19:5), lavishes his love on us (1 John 3:1), and rejoices over us with singing (Zeph. 3:17).

In short, the Father is the glorious raison d'être of restoration, welcoming all of his penitent children back to himself with a fatherly kiss and tender embrace (Luke 15:20).

....

For greater clarity, it is worth noting that the above three interconnected promises – namely, salvation through Christ, empowerment through the indwelling Spirit, and sonship to the Father – demonstrate that responsibility for delivering the promise of blessing to all peoples on earth lies squarely on the shoulders of all three members of the Godhead (Father, Son and Spirit), each with a different role in the administration and fulfilment of that blessing. It is also worth noting that, while we have focused here on the promise of blessing and how that translates into a New Testament context, there are also New Testament analogues relating to the Abrahamic promises of descendants and land. However, in a book primarily concerned with personal restoration in God, a steady spotlight is placed on that aspect of the Father's promise.

How Given: The Cast-iron Guarantee

Many years ago, a church youth leader and I agreed to take a group of teenagers to an activity centre in the Lake District of England for a holiday break and a bit of leisure and adventure. There were many outdoor activities to be enjoyed, including archery, kayaking, scrabbling up rivers and, as I recall, toppling like skittles into water (more of an unplanned activity). We hired a minibus for the trip and the hire contract was straightforward: a down payment was required up front, with the rest to be paid on return of the vehicle. This was not a loose arrangement between parties; it was a signed and legally binding contract. On returning the bus, however, we learned to our dismay that the hire company had seized full payment, without consent, from the youth leader's bank account during our time away. This action was both illegal and unethical, potentially tipping my friend's account balance into an unauthorised overdraft. Later, the company director came out to see us and apologised profusely for what he claimed had been failure on the part of an inexperienced employee to follow due procedure, offering us compensation by way of a free bus hire on our next church trip. In reality, it was not just a failure of procedure, it was a breach of contract. The meeting wound up amicably enough, with the two parties shaking hands over the offer of restitution, but the experience left me disinclined to use the company again.

The Father's Promise

My point in recounting the above story, is that fulfilment of a contract, in any sphere of life, is extremely important. Breaking a contract invariably leads to diminishment, if not eradication, of trust, often harming the reputation of the defaulter and damaging relations between the parties involved in the contract – this applies whether we are talking about a business contract (in this case a signed agreement), a retail contract (e.g., a warranty on purchased goods), a political contract (e.g., an election pledge), or a social contract (e.g., the principle that friends look out for one another). Keeping our promises, formal or informal, is vital to the cohesion of society – to families, communities and civilisation itself. This truth is not lost on God. In fact, there is no-one who watches over his word more intently to see it fulfilled than he does (Jer. 1:12). For this reason, God cut a blood covenant with Abraham, a customary means of ratifying an oath between parties in ancient times. This practice carried maximum legal and moral weight, and the liable party was obligated to make good on its oath, with serious repercussions for defaulting.

With this in mind, here is how the Abrahamic covenant took place, as described in Genesis 15: God instructed Abraham to sacrifice some animals, cut the larger ones in half, and lay the pieces on the ground in two parallel lines to form a makeshift walkway. In a normal transaction of this nature, the two parties coming into agreement would walk together between the pieces of the covenant, and the oath would be solemnly sworn by the promise-giver to the promise-receiver. However, this is not how the Abrahamic covenant unfolded. Following Abraham's efforts to shoo away some hungry birds that had swooped down to feed on the animal carcasses, God put Abraham into a deep sleep to prevent any further interference by him and shut him out of the rest of the covenant process. While Abraham was incapacitated, God passed between the covenant pieces alone, appearing as a smoking furnace and a flaming torch. God then issued a promise to Abraham, perfectly valid and effective, while Abraham remained helpless throughout the crowning stage of the ceremony. The promise was therefore issued without Abraham's input.

The significance of God's unilateral action here cannot be overstated. It is the key to understanding why God's promise to Abraham and all peoples on earth is not only good, it is unbreakable. God acted independently during the climactic stage of the Abrahamic covenant because his perfect promises rely wholly on himself (Heb. 6:13-14), resting on his own infallible word and innate trustworthiness. He does not need a helping hand in the design or execution of his impeccable plans, because sinful hearts are incapable of contributing to those plans. The Apostle Paul expressed this truth plainly as follows: *"When we were utterly helpless, Christ came at just the right time and died for us sinners"* (Rom. 5:6, NLT).

The inescapable fact is, that if we could undo the effects of the Fall by our own efforts, then Christ's death on the cross would be rendered meaningless (Gal. 2:21), as would all of God's plans and interventions. This is precisely why Paul, in his letter to the errant believers in Galatia, urged them to abandon self-righteous rule keeping and throw themselves back onto God's grace, which is freely extended to us through the death of Christ. God, in his wisdom, has provided us with a cast-iron guarantee of salvation in Christ, generously raining down from heaven and chasing after us with unbridled force. The only obstacles to this are those lying within our own resistant hearts.

How Received: Hearts Open to Heaven

There is a truism, which I have often heard repeated, that a gift unopened is a gift forfeited. Acts of ignoring or spurning a gift do not make it any less a gift; they simply deprive us of its rewards. The nature of the Father's gift of salvation to the world is that it is held out open-handedly from heaven and never forced on us. The Father is seeking out children who freely open

The Father's Promise

their hearts to his generosity, not mindless automatons. Love is a two-way street, built on reciprocated affections and bustling with possibilities. If our so-called love for God always feels like a chore, then frankly we are pursuing something (or someone) else. The gift of God is unearned, not a salary dispensed for duties performed (Rom. 4:4-8). The Father is looking for open-hearted responders, not builders of monuments to self-effort and self-virtue (Eph. 2:8-9).

The key to how we receive the Father's promise is, once again, apparent in the story of the Abrahamic covenant. After execution of his blood covenant with Abraham, God commanded him to keep the covenant. For this, God instructed Abraham to have his flesh cut with the mark of circumcision, and to have all males in his household follow suit (Gen. 17:9-14). This physical mark on the body was to serve as an outward sign that Abraham and his descendants were subject to God's covenant promises. Critically, God charged Abraham to uphold his end of the covenant by continuing the practice of circumcision *for the generations to come* (Gen. 17:9). An active and sustained response to God's covenant promises was thus required.

Now, two major covenants between God and Israel followed after the Abrahamic covenant: these are the Old Covenant and the New Covenant, named in this way because the latter would end up surpassing and replacing the former (see Hebrews 9 for deeper insight). The Old Covenant, also known as the Mosaic covenant, is centred on the Law of Moses, itself spearheaded by the Ten Commandments, and the New Covenant is an everlasting covenant centred on salvation in Christ. Compliance with law is prescribed under the Old Covenant, while faith in Christ is vital under the New Covenant. In addition, physical circumcision is mandatory under the terms of the Old Covenant, but under the terms of the New Covenant, a more profound type of circumcision is now required: circumcision of the heart (Rom. 2:28-29). While the nature of circumcision has fundamentally changed from the Old to New Covenant arrangements, shifting from external to internal, the obligation of circumcision persists because it is a requirement *for the generations to come.* The Old Covenant, ratified by animal sacrifices, requires an external symbol (physical circumcision) to mark out those operating under that covenant. The New Covenant, ratified by the once-and-for-all sacrifice of God's own Son (Heb. 10:10), requires more potent verification: the internal mark of a changed heart. This is the New Testament analogue to physical circumcision and is the reason why Paul asserts that a true Jew is one who praises God sincerely from the heart, and not someone who simply bears a physical mark on their flesh (Rom. 2:29).

The act of circumcision pertains to the cutting away of something. Under the Old Covenant, foreskins were cut away. Under the New Covenant, those turning their hearts back to Father God through his Son, Christ, have their old lives cut away. Their spirits once steeped in disobedience towards God (Eph. 2:1-3) are replaced with new ones (Ezek. 11:19, 36:26), vibrant with the reality of sonship (Gal. 4:6). Endowed with this new life, sons and daughters begin to co-operate with the Spirit in cutting away internal hindrances interfering with the expression of new life (Rom. 8:5-13, 12:1-2). These hindrances are the dying echoes of orphanness that still cling to the human soul, even after new birth in Christ. With the Father's help, his children are those being transformed from the inside out, and not those striving to get right with God from the outside in (Matt. 23:26). Their hearts are open to heaven, bearing the enduring mark of circumcision inside themselves as they press on to greater glory in God.

Chapter 5

In His Hands

Throughout history, God has communicated with us in diverse ways, speaking to us definitively in these last days by his Son (Heb. 1:1-2). During his earthly ministry, Jesus surprised people by persistently using parables in public, evoking rich visual imagery and captivating the hearts and imaginations of those who flocked to hear him. He used vivid storytelling to convey powerful truths to those whose hearts were open to God, while expertly veiling the same from those whose hearts were closed (Matt. 13:10-17). He was a breath of fresh air standing apart from the dull, regimented ranks of the religious leaders of his day (John 7:46). While these leaders nit-picked incessantly over matters of religious law, turning on public displays of virtue signalling while spiritually bankrupt within themselves (Matt. 23:27-28), Jesus astounded audiences with engaging stories of his heavenly Father and breath-taking displays of power. His reports of God's kingdom pulsated with life, and people were frequently in awe of him (Luke 5:26). He offered people a river of hope and refreshing (John 4:13-14), attracting large crowds (Matt. 4:25), while his critics offered the people a dust bowl of self-righteous posturing (Matt. 23:4).

As part of his vibrant communication strategy, God has also communicated, and continues to communicate, to people by way of illuminating and instructive dreams (Joel 2:28; Acts 2:17). For example, in Matthew's Gospel we learn that God gave Joseph a dream (Matt. 1:20-21). This followed Joseph's discovery that Mary, his betrothed, was carrying a child that was not his. In light of this, Joseph set his mind to annul his betrothal to Mary and quietly send her away. After setting his mind to do this, God gave Joseph a dream in which the angel of the Lord instructed him not to be afraid and go ahead with his marriage to Mary, assuring him that the child in her womb was a sovereign act of God's Spirit. Joseph was also charged with naming the child Jesus, being the one who would save people from their sins. This dream radically changed the course of Joseph's life, and indeed the course of human history.

One night as I slept, I had a vivid dream of my own that I have no doubt came from God. The dream came during an extremely low point in my life (as described in chapter 2 of this book) and was the first in a short sequence of dreams from God, occurring over a relatively narrow interval of time in my late twenties and early thirties.

In the first of three remarkable dreams – I will address the other two separately in the next two chapters – I was floating above a field and could see myself down below. I watched as I walked across the field in an attempt to reach a silhouetted figure in the distance. I could see that the figure was Jesus, hanging on the cross, but the distance required to reach him seemed daunting. As I ploughed towards the cross, a horde of grasping hands suddenly sprang up out of the ground and began pulling violently at my legs. I could no longer move forward and started to sink underground, as an increasing number of hands rose up to pull me down. When all seemed lost and the sea of hands was finally about to push me under, I heard myself crying out, 'Jesus, Jesus! Save me!' At this, I was instantly delivered from the grasping hands and transported to Christ on the cross. I was hovering in the air, close to him. With his face tilted to one side, I watched as a rivulet of blood flowed down from where his makeshift crown of thorns had pierced his head. Finally, I saw a tear glistening and running down his cheek.

Six critical aspects of this dream will be explored here in relation to themes of personal restoration:

- *The grasping hands* - the nature of our captivity to sin
- *Calling on the Lord* - salvation in the name of Jesus
- *Drawn to the cross* - the sacrificial death of Christ
- *The rivulet of blood* - the power of Christ's blood
- *Jesus close up* - drawing near to God
- *The glistening tear* - the compassion of Christ.

These themes will be considered in turn and will reinforce the wonderful truth that, in Christ, the Father has been working for us and not against us (Rom. 8:31).

In the Grip of Sin

I don't see why I should go to hell. I'm a good person and I've never murdered anyone.

Anonymous

I recently overheard the above comment, one I have heard expressed countless times over the years, or variations of such. It is a view that is very common and one that is perfectly reasonable to hold and articulate. Instinctively, many people recoil at the idea that a decent person rejecting Christ would be treated by God, at the Final Judgment, in exactly the same fashion as an unrepentant murderer. So, let me follow the trail of thought underlying the remark that I overheard and make a rational proposition: surely a fair-minded God would not treat good people in the same manner as evil people. This proposition was once put directly to the Lord by Abraham when he questioned the Lord's plan to wipe out the cities of Sodom and Gomorrah (Gen. 18:25).

Reflections of a Broken Son

To address this valid proposition, and to understand the true nature of sin itself, we need to go back and examine more thoroughly what happened at the Fall. Acting against the perfect counsel of God, Adam and Eve ate fruit from the Tree of Knowledge and their eyes were opened like God's, causing them to know both good and evil. Falling for the serpent's sly suggestion that God was limiting them, they pitched themselves paradoxically into a world of narrower horizons, with pain, toil and sweat constraining them in their new self-directed reality. Putting aside the fact that God mercifully restored them back to fellowship with himself, their inner lives were now corrupted. Though they were still capable of calling on the Lord and acquiring his help (Gen. 4:1), the tendency of their hearts, post-Fall, was largely to figure out what they thought was best for their own lives, for good or evil. Their son Cain exemplified this tendency when, driven by presumption rather than faith, he thought it best to present God with a self-styled offering, and then, after God rejected his offering, thought it best to vent his murderous rage on his brother, bludgeoning him to death in a field (the story of Cain and Abel is found in Genesis 4).

Now, here is where we get to the heart of the matter and where we can begin to see the true face of sin. The Tree of the Knowledge of Good and Evil essentially poisoned, and still poisons, the human soul in two different ways. On the side of evil, we find a world of obvious sins: murder, assault, lying, stealing, sexual depravity and generally any behaviour that manifestly hurts or defiles others, or self. (Cain's obvious and visible sin was murder.) On the side of so-called good, however, we encounter a murkier reality where sins are often imperceptible to those guilty of them: pride, self-righteousness, envy, greed and generally any attitude or action where we selfishly elevate our own needs above those of others, or trample others with the sense of our own rightness. (Cain's less obvious and unseen sin was pride.) In short, with all of humanity infected by the Tree of Knowledge, the side of evil hangs out plainly for all to see, while the side of 'good' is the silent killer lurking in the shadows. This is what makes sin truly insidious; it often escapes our notice because it so deftly hides within us (Rom. 7:9-11).

When we understand this toxic blend of 'good' and evil sins that has degraded human nature, itself a by-product of spiritual orphanness and estrangement from Father God, we can begin to understand why Jesus gave the so-called decent people of his day such a hard time. One incident sums up this point perfectly. One day, Jesus was sitting and eating with a band of people who were regarded locally, by some at any rate, as good-for-nothings and reprobates (this story is found in Luke 5:27-32). A group of religious leaders and experts of the law questioned Jesus for keeping such disreputable company, effectively casting doubt on his morals. Seeing through their ruse to trip him up and calling them out on their self-importance, Jesus informed them that sick people, not the well, needed a doctor, and that he had come for sinners and not the righteous. In their black-and-white universe, these critics of Jesus were the good guys (righteous) in their own eyes and those not aligned with them were the bad guys (sinners). The tragic part of adopting this stance was that their claim to be the enlightened ones was in fact self-delusional (John 9:41). The scary part was that, in the absence of authentic saving faith in God, Jesus knew that they would go on to die in their sins (John 8:24). This is precisely the dilemma of a human soul poisoned by the 'good' side of the Tree of Knowledge. It blinds us to our innate sinfulness and need of salvation.

Before my own encounter with Christ, I saw myself as a good person despite my habitual drinking, and some around me saw me in a similar light, at least those whom I did not hurt too badly. However, the truth was that I needed God as much as anyone else. Paul, in his letter to the Romans, roundly deprives us of the notion that any individual is better off than another in the matter of meeting God's standard (Rom. 3:9-20). With the exception of Christ himself whose heart was unblemished (Heb. 4:15; 1 John 3:5), sin is otherwise a universal condition and a leveller of humanity (Rom. 3:23). It is only our pride, and the blinkeredness stemming from feeding off the 'good' part of the Tree of Knowledge, that keeps us imprisoned in unknowing darkness. The human race is captive in the grip of sin, in both its 'good' and evil forms, whether or not we subscribe to that truth. This is what God was trying to convey to me in my dream of grasping hands. I was entangled in a force far greater than myself, a force woven into the very fabric of my being. He was showing me that I required external intervention to break free from sin's otherwise stubborn grip on my life; or, as Jesus succinctly put it, I needed a doctor (spiritually speaking).

One day, I will stand before a holy God to whom I am accountable, and I will need more than decency on that sober day. This effectively answers the remark that I heard about God's fairness and that was highlighted at the start of this section. Fortunately, mercy has triumphed over judgment (James 2:13), and hope is at hand for everyone, without exception, in the form of a beautiful and powerful name.

Name Above All Names

In biblical times, the meaning of people's names was considered as important, if not more important, than the simple act of ascribing names. Time and again in the Bible, children were named in quite literal ways for specific reasons. Reasons often included a way of praising God for a particular blessing given. For example, Eve named her son Seth (*appointed*) after God appointed the birth of a third child to her following the loss of her second child, Abel. Not all biblical names were this positive or celebratory. One of the most unfortunate names given to a child in the Scriptures was Ben-Oni (*son of my sorrow*), so named by Rachel, wife of Jacob, during her very painful labour in pregnancy and shortly before her death in childbirth (Gen. 35:16-18). Possibly wanting to spare his son barbed taunts in childhood playgrounds of the day or, more likely, simply opposed to the despondent name Ben-Oni, Jacob renamed his son Benjamin (*son of my right hand*).

This approach to naming children in a consciously meaningful way was still broadly practiced in Israel at the time of Jesus. When the Father sent his Son into this culture, he did not flout the naming convention of the day, instead embracing it with divine precision and forethought. The name Jesus, being the Greek form of the Hebrew name Yeshua, means *The Lord saves*. A couple of key points are worth noting concerning the naming of Jesus. First, human beings played no part in deciding on his name, with Mary and Joseph simply acting as faithful executors of God's sovereign instruction to name the child Jesus (Matt. 1:18-25). Second, the commanding angel conveying this instruction made it explicit that Jesus was to be so named because he would save his people from their sins. The implication of this is truly astounding since it was already established, long before Jesus' arrival, that only God could save people. The prophet Isaiah confirmed this truth:

> "I, even I, am the LORD, and apart from me there is no saviour."
>
> Isa. 43:11, NIVUK

The inescapable conclusion here is that Jesus was far more than the Lord's instrument on earth: he himself was the glorious Lord in the flesh (John 1:1,14), being the exact representation of his Father (Heb. 1:3). His name therefore carries all of the majesty and force that this revelation implies, attested by Paul in one of his most well-known proclamations concerning the pre-eminence of Jesus:

> *Therefore God exalted him to the highest place*
> *and gave him the name that is above every name,*

that at the name of Jesus every knee should bow, in heaven and on earth and under the earth, and every tongue acknowledge that Jesus Christ is Lord, to the glory of God the Father.

Phil. 2:9-11, NIVUK

The key to why Jesus' name is so powerful shines like a brilliant beacon in these verses: with finality and clear-sightedness, the Father elevated his Son to *the highest place.* After Jesus provided the remedy for our sins, the Father received him back to heaven and seated him at his right hand, announcing with gladness that this was his Son, victorious by his side (Heb. 1:5,13). There is no more exalted position to occupy, no loftier place to be reached, no greater honour to be bestowed, and no nobler title (*Son*) to be awarded. Jesus possesses the name above all names, and into his qualified and faithful hands the Father has placed all nations as an inheritance (Ps. 2:7-9).

At his name, demons flee in terror, believers are protected and equipped with spiritual gifts, and people are healed of their afflictions (Mark 16:17-18). At his name, signs and wonders are released and his word goes forth with boldness (Acts 4:30-31). Moreover, all who call on his name will be saved, with certainty and without exclusion (Rom. 10:13). His name pushes back the darkness, shatters strongholds and restores hope to broken lives, because it stems from the power of an indestructible life (Heb. 7:16). He is singularly unlike any other person who has lived, perfectly attuned to his Father's will (John 5:19), and no name given to the people of this world carries greater authority or weight (Eph. 1:18-23).

The Cross of Christ

Just as the name of Jesus was no accident, the cross of Christ was no mere coincidence either. The salvation of the human race was planned meticulously in heaven long before it appeared on earth. This ancient plan was encoded in the promise to Eve that her seed would crush the serpent's head, while the heel of the seed would be struck in turn (Gen. 3:15), the latter pronouncement anticipating the wounding of Jesus' heels during crucifixion. While the plan to rescue humanity was somewhat shrouded within the Edenic promise, the story of Abraham setting out to sacrifice his son Isaac on Mount Moriah, as told in Genesis 22, is the first occurrence in the Bible where God's salvation plan bursts into clear panoramic view. In this episode, the sacrificial death of Christ is forecast, like an airplane banner unfurled and stretching boldly between the Old and New Testaments.

In brief, the Lord God, in a test of Abraham's faith, commanded him to sacrifice his son Isaac, offering no explanation. Abraham, on the back of God's long-standing and well-proven love for him, chose not to waver in his trust in God (Rom. 4:19-20), believing that God would not welch on his promises and that Isaac would still be his heir despite the unsettling and confounding command. Abraham had witnessed his son Isaac born by supernatural means (Gen. 17:15-22) and he reasoned that God would also raise his son back up from the dead by supernatural means (Heb. 11:19).

Every amazing experience up until this moment had hardwired Abraham's trust in a God who was unfailingly for him and would keep his promises. In light of this, he set off for Mount Moriah to carry out the sacrifice, taking his son and two servants with him. Leaving the servants behind, Abraham and Isaac ascended the mountain alone. Seeing no sacrificial lamb in sight, Isaac inquired after its curious absence, to be told by his father that the Lord himself would provide the lamb for the burnt offering. At the appointed location, Abraham trussed his son and placed him on a makeshift altar. As he raised the knife to complete the sacrificial ceremony, God halted the proceedings and provided a ram in place of Isaac. In view of his exceptional faith, God promised Abraham countless descendants who would gain certain victory over their enemies.

Several strong parallels exist between this Old Testament story and the death of Jesus on Mount Calvary. First, both accounts involved sons assuming the role of sacrificial lamb. Moreover, Isaac carried the wood for the burnt offering (Gen. 22:6), while Christ bore the wooden cross to the place of his death (John 19:17). Another striking echo is found in God's decree of blessing to Abraham, with the Lord underscoring the fact that Abraham had not withheld from him his *only* son (Gen. 22:16) – his only son by his wife Sarah, that is. There is no loose remark at play here: the phrasing is precise and premeditated, with God purposefully alluding to his *only begotten* Son and signalling Christ's future once-and-for-all sacrifice. It is also worth noting that in both events the Lord provided the offering. Isaac was not required for sacrifice but only for proof of Abraham's faith, with God stepping in to provide the substantive sacrifice in the form of a ram. In the case of Christ, the Son himself was the sacrifice, choosing to redeem humanity by his own blood.

All of these parallels reveal that the salvation plan was carved out long before Christ walked the earth. The cross of Christ was always meant to happen, standing as the visceral yet stately bridge between a fallen people and a merciful God.

The Blood of the Lamb

To further understand the necessity of Christ's sacrifice and the shedding of his blood, it is useful to consider why the Old Covenant, ratified by the blood of animals, was superseded by the New Covenant, ratified by the blood of Christ. In Hebrews 9, the author, commonly believed to be Paul, lays out a compelling case for the change of covenants. The case for why the covenants had to be changed is addressed first, and the specific issue of blood is addressed afterwards.

The necessity for change essentially pivoted around a requirement to transition from dutiful adherence to law, to dynamic restoration of the human heart by the Spirit. The progression of covenants from old to new thus signifies a far-reaching change of the guard, so to speak, from ritual to renewal. In the previous chapter of this book, this issue was touched upon when the contrast between an outward mark of physical circumcision and an inward mark of heart circumcision was highlighted. This change of covenants, reflecting a fundamental shift from external to internal, was not some new-fangled idea dreamt up by the author of Hebrews to justify the Christian faith and pour scorn on the Old Covenant: the idea was in fact presaged by a number of Old Testament prophets, including Ezekiel (Ezek. 36:26-27), Joel (Joel. 2:28-29) and Zechariah (Zech. 12:10). Also, Jeremiah is particularly explicit regarding institution of the New Covenant:

> *'This is the covenant that I will make with the people of Israel after that time,'* declares the LORD.
>
> *'I will put my law in their minds and write it on their hearts. I will be their God, and they will be my people. No longer will they teach their neighbour, or say to one another, "Know the LORD," because they will all know me, from the least of them to the greatest,'* declares the LORD. *'For I will forgive their wickedness and will remember their sins no more.'*
>
> Jer. 31:33-34, NIVUK

In the above passage, we can see clearly why another covenant was required. The first one was only an interim measure, powerless to change people's hearts. The deep and pernicious roots of sin, arising from our disastrous exposure to the fruit of the Tree of Knowledge, required more radical treatment than mere outward compliance with law could ever provide. So, why bother having law at all? Paul, an expert on matters of law (Gal. 1:14), anticipates this question, verifying that the Law of Moses was a temporary measure put in place by God to safeguard humanity until the unveiling of salvation in Christ (Galatians 3:15-4:7 offers a lengthier view of Paul's reasoning). Basically, the law was a divine stopgap to prevent humanity from going off the rails until Jesus could come and finally overthrow sin by the sacrifice of himself. Hence, Paul compares the law to a little child's guardian (Gal. 4:1-5) and Jesus to the great deliverer who has ushered us, through faith in him, into maturity of sonship to the Father (Gal. 4:6-7).

In view of these weighty matters, the question now arises: why were the covenants ratified by blood? The answer lies, yet again, in the details of the Fall. While Adam and Eve still retained innocence, God strictly warned them to refrain from eating from the Tree of Knowledge, cautioning them that death would *certainly* result from such action (Gen. 2:17), a fixed consequence as inexorable as the law of gravity. While death here refers to physical death, above all it refers to spiritual death, that is, separation from God's holy presence. Piggybacking on sin, death stole into the human condition and we subsequently became subject to the entwined powers of sin and death (Rom. 5:12-14). Moreover, we remain under the control of sin and the related sentence of death until something opposite and greater than these primal forces arrives.

Thankfully, the grace (gift) of God in Christ is exactly this superior and counteracting force (Rom. 5:15-21). To understand why God's grace is truly amazing, as sung the world over, here is the crux of the matter: either a sinner bears the death sentence himself or herself, or logically something or someone else pays in lieu. However, to redeem the guilty – that is, to make due payment on their behalf – the replacement must be innocent, or a double payment would be incurred and the sacrifice rendered obsolete. For this reason, under the Old Covenant, the penalty of death was transferred onto innocent animals, and their blood, being proof of death, ensured that sinners were outwardly cleansed (Heb. 9:13) and fellowship with God resumed until further cleansing was required (Heb. 10:1-3).

Under the New Covenant, the blood of the spotless Lamb of God, Jesus Christ (John 1:29), has permanently torn down the powers of sin and death in a single enduring sacrifice (Heb. 9:25-26), wiping out the need for further sacrifice (Heb. 10:11-13). The blood of Christ is therefore part of a better covenant between God and humanity, permanently securing our freedom from sin and death, and further gifting us with an everlasting inheritance as God's children (Heb. 9:15).

Up Close and Personal

The part of my dream where I was instantly transported close up to Jesus after calling on his name, leans into one of the most crucial points that I want to raise in this book concerning personal restoration: the Father is after deep intimacy with his children. He yearns with all of his heart to recover what was lost in Eden through human folly and rebellion; that is, to have a close personal walk with us. The good news is that if we draw near to God, then he will certainly come close to us (James 4:8). Nearness to God is found in reliance upon him and not in self-reliance:

> *The person who lives in right relationship with God does it by embracing what God arranges for him. Doing things for God is the opposite of entering into what God does for you.*
>
> Gal. 3:11b, MSG

Reflections of a Broken Son

The truth is, God can do marvellous things in and through ordinary hearts yielded to him (Isa. 6:8; Gal. 2:20). This is a step-wise adventure of faith into an ever-increasing, intimate knowledge of God, accepting for now that we only know in part (1 Cor. 13:12).

The call to re-embrace intimacy with our heavenly Father, however, is difficult for hearts still hampered by orphaned sensibilities, and the temptation in our natural selves is to fall back instead on predictable and formulaic patterns of service to God. This was the error of the Galatian Christians that was touched on in the previous chapter. We are to embrace the promise of the Holy Spirit and walk in his renewing power (Gal. 5:16; Titus 3:5), choosing attentiveness to the Lord's voice (John 10:27) over empty, repetitive rituals (Isa. 1:11). Jesus rejected such sterility, being in perfect accord with his Father's will (John 5:19) and always sensitive to the promptings of the Spirit (Luke 4:1). This is what got him into frequent trouble with the religious leaders of his time: he dared to elevate and extol intimate knowledge of his Father over humdrum, rule-based religion (John 17:24-26).

While believers who lived during the period of the Old Testament did not have the benefit of the renewing Spirit residing within them, many still walked closely with God. Abraham is a prime example. The importance of his close walk with God is that he received his remarkable promises from God four hundred and thirty years prior to introduction of the Law of Moses (Gal. 3:17). This means, significantly, that Abraham did not possess law as a guiding compass for living. As a friend of God (James 2:23), all he possessed was childlike trust in his heavenly Father; and yet his simple faith was exactly what put him in right standing with God (Gen. 15:6; Rom. 4:22). Moses also understood the primacy of intimacy with God, despite being the person whom God used to usher in law. When Moses asked God to teach him his ways (Exo. 33:13), God did not instruct him to be a good law-abiding citizen:

In His Hands

The LORD replied, 'My Presence will go with you, and I will give you rest.'
                              Exo. 33:14, NIVUK

In turn, Moses replied to the Lord that he regarded his divine presence as a vital indication of God's favour upon his life, and further recognised that the Lord's presence was the distinctive mark of his chosen people, setting Israel apart from all other nations on the face of the earth (Exo. 33:16).

The pre-eminence of God's presence is a constant under the Old and New Covenants. Today, it is not moral virtue or charitable works that distinguish God's people – the body of Christ does not have a monopoly on morality or acts of kindness – it is the Spirit of God within, renovating people's lives from the inside out, that remains the touchstone of authentic Christian experience and witness (Rom. 8:9-11). As his people, we carry the Lord's presence (John 17:20-26), inhaling and exhaling that beautiful life only as we focus on God rather than on ourselves, adopting his selfless agenda rather than our own (John 7:18).

When churches lose sight of God's enlivening presence, instead falling back on rigid structures and behaviours like the Galatian Christians, they become dry wells, leaving people's lives untouched and unchanged. Lifeless rituals have never mended a broken heart but, through faith in Jesus Christ, the ingress of God's presence in the human heart becomes, with our co-operation, a never-ending and thriving wellspring of life (John 4:13-14).

The Compassionate Lord

Over the years, I have heard non-believing friends and acquaintances tell me that even if God was real, they felt disqualified to approach him on account of who they were and what they had done. This is misguided thinking. Our shortcomings, even our most shameful moments, in fact make us qualified to become God's children. Our mistakes are the very reason Jesus allowed whips, thorns and nails to pierce and rend his flesh (Isa. 53:5; 1 Pet. 3:18). He did not endure such pain for people with faultless lives and in no need of assistance. As already pointed out, Jesus came for sinners and not the righteous (Luke 5:32). When people discount themselves from God's kingdom, they underestimate the depths of Christ's compassion, failing to realise how tender-hearted the Saviour is and how readily accepting he is of all who turn to him, regardless of their history (John 6:37).

Among the stories in the Bible depicting Jesus' compassion, one springs to mind when I consider this subject. The story is found in John 8:1-11. It tells of a woman caught red-handed in adultery, who was dragged publicly before Jesus by religious leaders. Riddled with deceit and dripping with insincerity, they came to get Jesus' verdict on the woman's appropriate punishment, as per law. Superficially, they deferred to Jesus' wisdom, secretly hoping to wrong-foot him and acquire grounds for accusing him. Spurred by a harsh interpretation of law, they had already made up their own minds regarding the woman's punishment, coming armed with stones and ready to kill her. Jesus, seeing through their duplicity, remained silent and wrote on the ground. (One tradition has suggested that Jesus etched the specific sins of the assembled accusers in the dirt.)

When ready to speak, he threw out an uncompromising challenge to these angry men, inviting any one of them who had no sin to be the first to cast a stone at the woman. With this razor-sharp word, Jesus cut through their charade and exposed their hypocrisy. One by one, the accusers shuffled away in humiliation. Turning to the woman, he asked her if anyone was left to condemn her. When she replied that no-one was left, Jesus told her that he did not condemn her either, instructing her graciously to be on her way and cautioning her to sin no more.

Here we see the clear contrast between two very different standpoints: fault-finding religion versus divine compassion.

In His Hands

Rule-based religion, at its most unbending and pitiless, promotes obsession with others' sins, inciting disapproval of those who are perceived to break the rules, while blinding its devotees to their own failings and missteps (Luke 6:37-42). At worst, this perverted outlook, motivated by an obscene underlying spirit, can lead to the callous treatment, or even execution, of those who deviate from the rules (John 8:42-44). The problem of heartless religious practices, being in force when Jesus walked the earth and still evident today, stretches all the way back to Cain who murdered Abel, because his self-righteous actions were rejected by God, while the righteous actions of his brother were accepted (1 John 3:12).

The difference between Jesus and his religious critics essentially boils down to the distinction between a tender and a hard heart. The Lord is deeply merciful (2 Sam. 24:14) and he calls us to live in that same quality of mercy (Luke 6:36). He is not the perpetually stern figure painted by some who have used that depiction of God as a cover for their own anger and hatred. The compassion of God in Christ is boundless, wiping the slate clean in our lives (Rom. 8:1) and giving us a fresh start every day (Lam. 3:22-23). With relentless love, God reaches out to us with his tender mercies (Isa. 54:10; Luke 1:76-79), cheering us on and enabling us, with our compliance, to reach our full potential in him (Jer. 29:11; Phil. 4:13). His love for us is epic and impossible to measure or contain (Rom. 8:37-39). Moreover, he imbues us with everlasting life and takes us into his beautiful hands, out of which we can never be snatched (John 10:28). He is the compassionate Lord who loves us like no-one else ever has and no-one else ever will.

Reflections of a Broken Son

Chapter 6

Death of a Superhero

I have been married to my wife Lesley now for over 20 years. We share a great number of common interests, but I have one no-go area in my life that is a little secluded 'bunker' that I alone occupy, where I can blissfully pander to my inner geek. This is my hobby stretching back to childhood: reading and collecting American superhero comics. I have three boxes of comics sitting proudly on top of my wardrobe, which my wife occasionally casts a grimace towards, that is if she even registers them at all. The kindest thing that she has ever said about my hobby was that, if I was unwilling to burn my stash of comics like a good supportive husband would, then I could at least keep the offending articles out of her way. In view of this loving concession, my hobby feels like a dirty secret, but at least I get to retreat to my delightful bunker whenever she is watching her mind-numbing trash on the TV. (I tried to be charitable here, but the truth will out.)

In the last chapter, I spoke about Father God communicating to his children through dreams. A short number of years following my dream about Christ on the cross, God released another dream into my heart one night, conveying powerful truths to me within a lively superhero narrative. Like a parable in dream format and using imagery that I could appreciate, this was the most unusual of the three dreams that God gave to me, jam-packed with dramatic incidents and vibrant colours.

Where the first dream of the cross had set out essential truths about what the Father has accomplished for us through the sacrificial death of his Son, this second dream was about to paint a vivid picture of the response required of me in the face of salvation in Christ. Though there is nothing for anyone to add to Christ's perfect and completed work of redemption (John 17:4), just as Abraham had nothing to add when God passed alone between the covenant pieces, salvation properly received demands works of faith (James 2:14-26) as opposed to works of the law (Rom. 3:27-28; Gal. 3:1-5), and God was now ready to show me the path forward.

In the dream, I saw myself dressed in a gaudy superhero costume, replete with cape. As I gauged my surroundings, I saw that I was trapped in a run-down and shadowy domed city. The denizens of the city were attired in sackcloth and their faces were bleak and etched with sadness. With mounting alarm, I realised that I needed to break out of this prison. Bracing myself, I leapt off the ground and flew into the air, set on smashing through the dome-shaped barrier that surrounded the city. Like a streak of red crayon scarring a dark sky, I raced towards freedom. Blocking my way, a swarm of winged gorillas suddenly appeared, covered with purple fur and baring cutthroat fangs. An aerial battle ensued, and I fought hard with the ruthless creatures before being pounded back to the ground. Then, with even greater force than before, I launched myself skyward into another frenzied dog-fight, only to be hammered to the ground yet again. This scenario played out several times, on each occasion yielding the same frustrating outcome, no matter the degree of resolve on my part.

Running out of energy after numerous attempts to escape, I mustered up the strength for one last big push. With grim determination, I sprang off the ground once again. This time, I

Death of a Superhero

sped past my winged adversaries as if they were caught in freeze-frame. I continued climbing aloft, expecting freedom to follow shortly. As I rose higher, however, the sky grew darker and the air turned disturbingly cold. A sense of dread gripped my heart. Peering into the gloom, I suddenly saw a tight-knit formation of icy blue gorillas zooming towards me. These new beasts were fiercer looking than their purple relatives, clearly higher up the food chain and more disciplined. At the mere sight of these sinister creatures, I made a tactical, self-preserving decision: I sped back to the ground as fast as I had risen and collapsed onto my knees. I was down for the last time, broken and exhausted.

As I knelt in defeat, I began weeping. Tears ran freely down my face and over my costume. I watched as the garish outfit dissolved, washed away in a flood of grief, until I was stripped bare. My alter ego was gone; dead and buried. Still kneeling and in a state of vulnerability, a large hand suddenly appeared, scooping me up into its expansive embrace. For a considerable length of time, the mysterious hand carried me along the main street of the enclosed city, hurtling past the captive citizens in an unstoppable forward drive. At some point, it veered upwards like a rocket in an abrupt change of pace and direction. Approaching the dome at great speed, I saw that the barrier was a shiny black membrane. Instinctively, I lifted my hand to cut through the skin-like structure only to discover another hand, the partner of the one lifting me, brushing my hand away purposefully. The correcting hand then struck the dome in a slicing motion, rupturing the membrane. In that moment, a brilliant burst of sunshine flooded my vision and the intense light caused me to wake up, startled and gasping.

This dream may seem like a bizarre plot from some B-movie but, beneath the surface, I have realised over many years that God was showing me a blueprint for properly relating and responding to his divine initiatives. In this context, there are four specific elements of the superhero dream that I want to explore in this chapter:

- *Striking for freedom*   - finding freedom in God's purpose for our lives
- *Rising and falling*   - getting in the way of God's purpose for our lives
- *Resting in his hands*   - the necessity of entering God's rest
- *Breaking into light*   - living in abundant life through Christ.

In the reflections that follow, we will see that the Father intends for us to prosper in this life, secure in his provisions (Phil. 4:19).

Freedom in Purpose

> *'For I know the plans I have for you,' declares the* LORD, *'plans to prosper you and not to harm you, plans to give you hope and a future.'*
>
> Jer. 29:11, NIVUK

Our heavenly Father wants us to have glorious purpose in life. We are not, as some have argued, products of biochemical happenstance that blindly crawled out of some primeval marsh. On the contrary, there is a nurturing God who breathes life into us (Gen. 2:7), shapes us in our mothers' wombs and declares rich potential over our lives (Jer. 1:5; Gal. 1:15-16). Far from being accidental, we are fearfully and wonderfully made (Ps. 139:14). With our hearts open to heaven, we will discover that God only harbours good intentions towards us (Exo. 33:19; Matt. 7:11), inviting us to taste what he has to offer (Ps. 34:8) and enjoy the rewards of his great favour towards us in Christ (Eph. 1:3-10). In concordance with this view, Jesus spoke of his intent to enrichen our lives, while highlighting the opposing intent of Satan:

> *"The thief's purpose is to steal and kill and destroy. My purpose is to give them a rich and satisfying life."*
>
> John 10:10, NLT

Three years ago, my family and I attended a Christian conference held at the Scottish Event Campus in Glasgow. Over a sunny weekend in July, there was contemporary worship, guest speakers, riverside walks and activities for kids. During the main conference proceedings and various seminars, speaker after speaker stressed the need to find a clear purpose in God, a theme advocated so passionately over the two-day event that I felt the Holy Spirit carving words deeply into my heart and then, just for good measure, highlighting them with a fluorescent pen. If there was a single sentence summing up the entire experience, it was one spoken by a key speaker, which I wrote down in my journal at the time: 'We have got one life, so make it worth living!'

On the back of this inspirational event, my wife and I sat down one evening and had a heart-to-heart discussion about how we wanted to respond to what we had heard about finding purpose in God. In conversation, we discovered that we were both thirsty for spiritual adventure. We had a mutual passion to step beyond our limitations at that time, and with the power of the Spirit to break free from a drifting and pedestrian existence – in the context of the superhero dream, the possibility of settling for mediocrity was our domed city. Having witnessed extraordinary answers to prayer (more of that later), we had known for some time that the miracles and exciting occurrences depicted in the Book of Acts were still relevant for today; but we also knew that the cost of stepping into that reality was to leave behind compromise and our respective comfort zones.

Reflections of a Broken Son

Following this newfound resolve, my wife and I ended up attending another two-day event focused on inner healing at a Glasgow church in September 2017. Over the course of the event, we submitted ourselves to God with a view to clearing out hindrances to faith, including unforgiveness, unbeliefs and the hurts carried from past negative experiences. Serious encumbrances to our walk with God were dealt with that weekend, with unwanted inner baggage cast off and thrown down a deep hole with God's help.

Looking back, I can see that this moment was key to entering into a place of deeper spiritual purpose and freedom, opening up opportunities to serve God that had previously been out of reach. This included becoming part of the church team that delivered the teaching on inner healing. With levels of anxiety significantly reduced after dealing with some underlying roots, I was also emboldened to undertake public speaking and share my faith, with an especially strong desire to help others find a way out of fear and anxiety. Openings for this arose when I was invited to speak at the church I belong to. The writing of this book can also be traced back to the weekend of inner healing, because I realise that, without that intervention, I would not have been sufficiently freed up to write down all of these experiences. Finally, this loosening of the heart further laid down the groundwork for an extraordinary encounter with God two years ago, which profoundly impacted my mental health in the most positive way imaginable. (I will describe that experience in chapter 8.)

In conclusion, God will grant us a sense of purpose, and a deep satisfaction in life, when we get rid of any internal junk that we may still carry (Ezek. 36:25; 1 John 1:9), and allow the Holy Spirit to touch and heal our wounds (Ps. 147:3; Jer. 30:17). The Spirit is always the great enabler, but he needs our consent and co-operation to break our unhelpful ties to the past and embrace a bold future in God.

Death of a Superhero

Hindering God's Purpose

If you were to ask Christians what they considered to be the greatest hindrance to their rightful inheritance in Christ, I would imagine that some might point a self-assured finger at the devil. Spiteful and obstructive though he is, my own unhesitating response would be to point an equally self-assured finger back at myself. This would not be an act of self-accusation; it would be an admission that I present a bigger potential threat to my rightful inheritance in Christ than a defeated enemy (Col. 2:15). The problem that I am alluding to here is one that I often refer to as *self on the throne*. This problem extends back to Eve's foolish strike for self-government in the Garden of Eden, and is thornier and more deeply entrenched in human nature than has commonly been recognised or conceded. (I speak for myself.) Let me illustrate here using an example, once again, from the life of Abraham.

Abraham was given an unsinkable promise by God of acquiring a son who would be his heir (Gen. 15:4). Being divinely preordained, the birth of a son (Isaac) brought about by the design and undertaking of God was inevitable. Between the issue and fulfilment of the promise, however, Abraham temporarily fell off the faith wagon and embarked on an ill-thought-out and self-appointed detour. Though he still believed in the substance of God's promise, he took charge of its execution when he sought to sire an heir for himself through his wife Sarah's maidservant, Hagar (Gen. 16:1-4). Here is the main point: no-one, including Abraham the mighty man of faith, is exempt from resorting to self-effort to get the results in life that they want (in this case an heir). The problem of striving in the flesh (relying on self), as opposed to walking in the Spirit (relying on God), is pervasive. This is the legacy of the Fall, and no-one is immune.

Reflections of a Broken Son

In Abraham's case, he did not need the devil to obstruct him in the matter of God's purpose for his life; his own fallen tendencies were enough to blindside him. Given the impossibility of Sarah naturally conceiving, Abraham's decision to take matters into his own hands and have a son (Ishmael) by Hagar was understandable, but counterproductive. What he failed to grasp was the inexorability of an all-powerful God capable of making the impossible possible (Jer. 32:17; Matt. 19:26).

In my own life, there has been a dogged pattern of trying to commandeer God's promise to restore my life. I have lost count of the number of times I have done that. I have equally lost count of how many times that the Father has stepped in graciously to amend my striving ways, but one incident stands tall in the catalogue of God's course-correcting interventions in my life. The following incident is tribute to a Father who disciplines his children in love, rather than with a harsh hand.

One day, in October 2017, I began a food fast, ingesting only liquids. I was fired up after attending the inner healing weekend a short while earlier and reasoned that if Daniel had prayed and fasted for twenty-one days for a breakthrough (Dan. 10:2-3), then so should I. On the sixth day of my self-appointed fast, I woke up to find myself feeling terribly ill. Shaky and fatigued, I thought that I was going down with a bad case of flu. By late afternoon, I retired to bed in the hope that a solid rest might shake off the ill feelings. Half an hour later, my wife shouted through to remind me that I needed to take our oldest daughter Rachel to work. As I rose out of bed, I suddenly experienced a sharp stabbing pain in my chest. The pain was excruciating and I panicked, briefly entertaining the notion that I was having a heart attack. The piercing sensation quickly subsided, however, and I was able to compose myself and take my daughter to work. As we approached the car, the solitary word *harm* dropped unexpectedly into my thoughts, but I was unable to process what I had sensed until later.

Death of a Superhero

Back home, after dropping my daughter off, I returned to bed for that now much needed rest. Remembering that the word *harm* had earlier intruded on my thoughts, it occurred to me to ask God if he had been trying to warn me about something. Recognising that God had not called me to fast, I conceded the possibility that I might have been harming myself. As such, I asked God to give me a fool-proof sign that I needed to stop fasting, to confirm that my actions were not in line with his will.

Twenty minutes later while still praying in bed, I heard a knock at the door. Downstairs I heard my son David answer the door and a deep male voice announcing, 'This is for you, mate!' There was no further exchange as I heard the door shut. As it was late in October, my first thought was that a Christmas purchase had arrived. I sprang out of bed to investigate, only to find my wife proceeding down the stairs in front of me, equally curious to see what had been delivered. I heard Lesley ask David, 'What's that in your hands, son?' The puzzled response came back, 'I don't know mum, but it's hot!' As I stared at David, I could see clearly that he was holding a takeaway meal in his hand. My wife and I ran to the door to tell the delivery man that there had been a mistake. Though it had been no more than a minute since David had shut the front door, the man was now nowhere to be seen. He had promptly vanished.

Closing the door, I turned round to look at my son again. At that moment, the proverbial penny dropped like a grand piano on my slow-witted senses. Here was the idiot-proof sign that I had asked for, not more than half an hour ago, in the form of a takeaway meal (by this point I could smell Chinese food). With no money asked for, no receipt provided, and no indication of where the meal or the man had come from, I surmised that God had granted me divine verification with bullhorn conclusiveness. Regardless of whether or not human error had occurred, the precise nature and timing of the delivery, along with the bizarreness and uniqueness of the situation, left me in no doubt that all of this went far beyond coincidence.

Reflections of a Broken Son

Recounting the story to my wife, I asked her politely, 'I think that this is a clear sign from God to break my fast, so can I eat this?' To which my wife, by now laughing, replied, 'Yes, go for it!'

Sitting at the kitchen table, my wife and I enjoyed the delicious food, with enough left over to give David and one of his friends a treat as well. After laughing, chatting and praising God for his kindness and generosity, Lesley left the kitchen after finishing the meal. As I got up to leave too, I sensed that the Father wanted to reveal something to my heart. As I stood still, waiting expectantly, the Spirit downloaded a revelation onto my heart, the gist of which was as follows (I have since added biblical references to support the truth of what was revealed to me):

> *Chill out, son! [Matt. 11:28-30] Pack in the religious performance and striving. You're trying to gain my approval and earn favour through fasting and other religious observances. Your self-appointed actions do not impress me one bit. [Isa. 58:5] My mercy is freely given and my love can never be earned. [Eph. 2:8-9] If they could be earned by good works, then my Son Jesus would not have had to die on a cross to pay for your sins. [Gal. 2:21] My gifts can only be received as gifts, unrelated to virtue, performance or any other kind of merit on your part. I provide for all of my children on the basis of my grace, so stop striving in your own terms. My love is extravagant and given to you on the basis that you are my child. [Gal. 4:6-7] Enjoy my goodness and provisions, which are freely and graciously yours as part of my family. [Eph. 1:3-6] Learn to rest in my presence. [Exo. 33:14]*

This was a defining moment for me. It killed something pernicious in my heart that had been eating away at my spiritual wellbeing for a long time. Like Abraham, we are to rest in God's promises and avoid grabbing the steering wheel to get the job done. In pursuit of genuine faith in God, we need to be clear about the distinction between self-generated and Spirit-led actions (Ps. 127:1; Zech. 4:6). Failure to exercise due care in this matter can lead to purely human enterprise masquerading as spiritual endeavour, even unbeknownst to ourselves (Jer. 17:9). If we want to lay hold of the abundant life that God has to offer (Ps. 36:8; 2 Cor. 9:8), our lives need to be governed by God's Spirit (Rom. 8:14), not simply by the next good idea that pops into our heads. If we place our trust firmly in God, he will show us that his promises are better delivered by his own good and capable hands, delivering blessings far beyond anything that we can ever imagine (Eph. 3:20).

Entering God's Rest

One day as I drove to work, in January 2018, I was praying in the Spirit (Rom. 8:26) when God spoke to my heart. A Spirit-breathed interjection pressed its way through my thoughts: *I need you to enter my rest.* I stopped praying for a few minutes to take in the significance of what I had just heard. Three things immediately occurred to me: first, the phrase, *I need you to*, gave the mysterious directive an insistency that elevated it beyond mere suggestion; second, I was unclear at that time about the full meaning of God's rest; and third, I was also at a loss concerning the means of entering something that I did not fully understand. In short, I was flummoxed but knew that something of great import had been conveyed to me by the Holy Spirit. In view of this, I prayed to God to clarify what his rest meant and the steps to entering it.

(On later reflection, I realised that the earlier Chinese meal incident had been a glimpse into God's rest, and that God had already been sowing the seeds of what it meant to rest in him in a practical way; but now he was about to radically expand my understanding of both the principle and necessity of entering his rest. In my walk with God, I have found that experience precedes understanding as frequently as the other way around, and is an essential tool to aid understanding.)

On the back of the call from God to enter his rest, I embarked on an in-depth study of the Book of Hebrews over a three-month period. Reading this book on a near-daily basis, a picture of God's rest began to unfold as the Spirit opened up the eyes of my heart. Before sharing some insights, it behoves me to point out that God's rest is a massive concept, a wide frontier of possibility arising from exercising a deep personal trust in God. I have only explored the edges of this frontier. With that said, I offer a few reflections here on what I have discovered so far about God's rest.

The first thing that God impressed on me was that the call to enter his rest is of the utmost priority:

> *God's promise of entering his rest still stands, so we ought to tremble with fear that some of you might fail to experience it.*
>
> Heb. 4:1, NLT

The fact that we are to fear the possibility of missing out on God's rest, even as Spirit-filled believers, should give us serious pause for thought. Here is my take on it: if some spiritual experience is so vital that we are to tremble with fear at the prospect of failing to enter it, then surely it is complete folly to push it down our to-do list, or even to strike it off the list altogether. This is not a minor or even second priority in God's kingdom; it is a matter of urgency, determining the quality of our walk with God and our effectiveness in service to him. Those who enter God's rest will be immeasurably more fruitful in everything that they do, as opposed to those who strive in their own strength to achieve the same results. Not only will the latter group of people accomplish lesser results, they may fail completely:

Death of a Superhero

If GOD doesn't build the house,
  the builders only build shacks.
If GOD doesn't guard the city,
  the night watchman might as well nap.
It's useless to rise early and go to bed late,
  and work your worried fingers to the bone.
Don't you know he enjoys
  giving rest to those he loves?
                    Ps. 127:1-2, MSG

Faith in God is the key that unlocks the door into his rest, and unbelief is the deadlock that bars our way (Heb. 4:1-3). Focusing on his goodness and abilities, rather than on ourselves, is our route of access. Moreover, we are to enter God's rest today (Heb. 4:7); not later, not next week, not even tomorrow – *today!* This means that God's rest is to be assimilated into our daily existence. In addition, it is neither laziness nor inaction; it is rest from labours borne out of human striving rather than genuine faith (Heb. 4:10). We are still to love, pray, witness, serve and encourage others – but we are to do so with a relaxed and settled attitude, knowing that it is God who equips us, breathes life into hearts and situations, and assumes responsibility for the outcome. Putting it another way, the way of Hagar (self-reliance) is invariably the path to futility and diminishing returns, while the way of Sarah (God-reliance) is invariably the path to freedom and bountiful living (see Galatians 4:21-31 for deeper insight into these principles). Resting in the hand of the Lord is our birthright as his children, and the doorway into greater experience of victory in him.

Abundant Life in Christ

At the time of studying God's rest, the Spirit spoke to me one Sunday morning in church, releasing another encouraging word into my heart. During worship, the voice of Jesus chimed deeply and reassuringly in my spirit: *I am match-fit to meet all of your needs*. This was a spark that lit a fire in my heart, bringing fresh perspective to my study of Hebrews and other books of the Bible, and causing me to notice things that I had failed to spot before. Above all, my attention was drawn to Jesus' unique aptitude and readiness to meet all of our needs (Ps. 84:11; Heb. 4:16).

Looking back, I am struck by the realisation that God had deliberately brought this theme to my mind while I was still meditating on the subject of his rest. I can see now that the connection between the two concepts is straightforward: those who enter God's rest, trusting in him for their needs to be met, will find fulfilment on a divinely industrial scale, impossible to attain by human effort (John 15:5). Jesus is not just content to pour a trickle of life into us; he desires to inundate us with abundant life (Ps. 16:11; John 10:10). So, while we might make significant material gains in this life through our own ingenuities and resourcefulness, we risk forfeiting everything else (James 1:11). Ironically, God will meet our material needs, gladly blessing us in that area of our lives as we place him front and centre (Matt. 6:33).

On hearing in my spirit that Jesus was *match-fit* to meet all of my needs, he opened up the Scriptures to furnish me with several compelling reasons as to why he is the only contender for the job. He alone can fulfil all of our needs because:

He is the Son of God: The most vital qualification that Jesus possesses to meet all of our needs is that he is divine. The Apostle John is unequivocal about this truth, opening his gospel with a bold description of Jesus as the Word of God (*the expression of the divine*) who lived in eternity with his Father before creation (John 1:1-2), and was instrumental in the formation of the universe (John 1:3). His life is an inextinguishable flame, igniting and illuminating human hearts (John 1:4-5). He effects deep inward change in those who put their trust in him, establishing their rightful status as children of

God (John 1:12-13). Moreover, he has entered into human experience (John 1:14), preceding and surpassing all who have ever lived (John 1:15), and bestowing us with one gracious gift after another (John 1:16). He is the unique Son who reveals to us the heavenly Father with whom he enjoys the closest relationship (John 1:18).

He is the Son of Man: The author of Hebrews, while also highlighting the divinity of Christ (Heb. 1:1-14), underlines his humanity (Heb. 2:5-18), offering deep insight into reasons why he clothed himself with human flesh. For a start, Jesus had to absorb death into himself to break its ruinous hold over us (Heb. 2:14-15), a task unachievable from a remote, deathless platform in eternity. As such, he took on human form to preside as mediator between God and people (Heb. 9:15). In him, humanity and divinity converged in love, wiping out the debt of our sins (1 Pet. 1:18-19) and swallowing up death (Isa. 25:7-8). Moreover, he knows what it is to suffer and be tempted (Heb. 2:18), being aware of human needs and limitations from an involved standpoint (Heb. 4:15-16). He is not some cosmic entomologist observing insects with cool forensic detachment. In simple terms, Jesus understands us because he became one of us.

He is a man of action: In a world where words are often cheap, there is a God who goes against the grain:

> *For the Kingdom of God is not just a lot of talk;*
> *it is living by God's power.*
> 1 Cor. 4:20, NLT

He has proved these words over and over again in my life, but he does not impose this reality on us; it comes through a willingness to take the plunge and discover the Lord's goodness for ourselves (Ps. 34:8). Jesus was a man of action first, whose teachings came on the back of astonishing displays of God's power (Acts 1:1). This is why people flocked to see him in their droves:

Reflections of a Broken Son

Everyone tried to touch him, because healing power went out from him, and he healed everyone.
Luke 6:19 NLT

Today, he still touches our lives with resurrection power (Rom. 6:4; Eph. 1:19-20), forgiving us for our sins (Ps. 103:3; Matt. 9:1-8), restoring hope to the broken-hearted (Ps. 147:3; Isa. 57:15), and continuing to heal us with his matchless power (Isa. 53:5; 1 Pet. 2:24).

He gives us everything: Christ did not have a single compromising bone in his body: he descended from heaven to earth to carry out his Father's will faithfully (John 6:38). This meant pressing on to finish the work of redemption (John 19:30), refusing temptations on the way (Matt. 4:1-11), and pushing through fierce opposition (Ps. 3:6) and anguish (Matt. 26:39). All of these facts together, present the picture of a man whose undeviating purpose was to complete the task assigned to him by his heavenly Father (Isa. 50:7; John 4:34). In the final analysis, he proved his love towards us conclusively:

> *Greater love has no one than this: to lay down one's life for one's friends.*
> John 15:13, NIVUK

The scars that he still bears on his hands and feet, following his resurrection, are testament to that fact (Luke 24:39). In light of all this, an important question arises for believers: if he has given us his own life when we were his enemies, what will he not give us now that we are his friends? (Rom. 5:10).

He is our high priest forever: Under the Old Covenant, the most important duty of the high priest was to conduct service once a year on the Day of Atonement, making atonement for himself and the people of Israel for all sins committed in the past year (Exo. 30:10). Two constraints weighed down this arrangement: first, death prevented high priests from remaining in office (Heb. 7:23); second, high priests needed to attend to their own failings before addressing those of the people (Heb. 7:27). Jesus eradicates these limits, now stepping permanently into the role of high priest on the basis of an unchangeable oath by God (Heb. 7:20-21). He acts as perfect mediator between a holy God and a fallen people, having made atonement for sin through the sacrifice of himself (Heb. 7:27). His priestly office is founded on an indestructible life (Heb. 7:16) and the salvation that he offers is complete (Heb. 7:25). He loves us like no other, working tirelessly on our behalf to see us restored and made whole (1 Thess. 5:23-24).

....

For all of the above reasons and more, Jesus is the light of the world (John 8:12). He invites us to come into his light and not just to observe it from a distance (John 3:21). While we try to make ends meet in this life, there is a God who want us to flourish and succeed (Gen. 39:2-5). I cannot claim to have mined the depths of all that God has to offer, because his love and the possibilities of thriving in him are boundless (Rom. 8:37-39). He waits for us to make a move (James 4:8), to lift up our eyes and willingly receive help from him (Ps. 121:1-2). He is ready to bless us in ways that are beyond anything that we could work out for ourselves (Phil. 4:13); and all who open up their hearts to him will not be disappointed (Ps. 22:5; Rom. 10:11).

Reflections of a Broken Son

Chapter 7

Turning Up the Heat

Labels to describe people are as unhelpful as they are helpful. The label *Christian*, for example, carries as many negative as positive connotations for people outside of church circles. Though I try not to hide who I am, I prefer these days not to throw out labels quickly or willy-nilly, choosing to relate to people in a label-free fashion until the subject of faith naturally arises, or I am moved to disclose something by the Spirit. This is not a hard-and-fast rule; it is a deliberate choice on my part to relate to others beyond the limitations of labels, or at least earn people's trust before using them in conversation.

I recall many years ago receiving a withering response on telling someone that I was a Christian, along the following lines: 'You Christians and your <expletive> hotline to God!' This sharp reaction came on the back of a courteous answer to a query about my beliefs. (To this day, I wonder what my critic would have said had I told him that I believed in robbing banks and hitting senior citizens like himself for sport. I may have got a better response than the one I did. I knew the person well enough though, and took no offence at his cynicism; just one of his many winsome qualities.) Underlying the cutting remark about Christians and their hotline to God was a perception of Christians as self-righteous hypocrites. The hotline – if that is how it is to be described – is only open, however, to those who humbly admit to their failings, not to the self-entitled or elite (Ps. 18:27; James 4:6). Jesus came for sinners, not the righteous (Matt. 9:13).

On the subject of hotlines, the whole concept of connecting to God was about to be opened up to me in a third dream, following the dreams about the cross and the worn-out superhero. There was a definite sequence to these dreams, choreographed by Father God and pivoting around one central theme: relationship with him. The first dream revealed that access to God had been made possible through the sacrifice of Jesus, and the second indicated that the nature of any meaningful relationship with God was one of continual reliance on him. The third was about to elucidate on matters of approaching God and experiencing his presence.

On the evening of my third nocturnal dream from God, I arrived early at church, two hours before a prayer meeting. Finding myself alone, I began praying fervently. Still suffering from bouts of acute anxiety at that time, I put aside my afflictions and cast my cares on God for the next hour. Pacing around the church sanctuary, I prayed to God for direction. After a time of calling on him and running out of ways to ask him for a clear path forward, I switched to praying in the Spirit, a means of allowing the Spirit of God to make intercession through me (Rom. 8:26-27). About twenty minutes or so into this activity, a fearfulness unexpectedly sprang up inside me, not unlike the panic attack that I had experienced a few years back. My head ordered me to cease praying, but my heart defied this mandate, instead urging me to press on.

As I pushed through a blizzard of fear with the help of the Spirit, a breakthrough came without warning. Like an elastic band stretched to breaking point, I felt the fear snap decisively inside me, and what felt like a heavy blanket was hauled perceptibly out of my body. Inwardly, there was an eruption of peace,

Turning Up the Heat

streaming out from my gut like a rush of warm water and filling me from head to toe. A river of peace had burst its banks inside me, sweeping away fear and anxiety in its irresistible wake. As the peace consumed me, I could not contain my excitement, praising God noisily in the empty room until my strength was spent. An indescribable joy pervaded my heart for an hour, and I felt as if the Lord's rapture had arrived early.

By the start of the prayer meeting, however, the amazing feeling of peace had faded, and with great disappointment I sensed that the gnawing anxiety had returned. Back home after the meeting, I felt angry towards God and let him know about my true feelings with a no-holds-barred prayer. I wept bitterly and told him that it felt cruel to have tasted such exquisite peace, only to have it taken away. After venting my anger for a considerable time, I drifted off into a deep sleep, still feeling badly let down by God.

As I slept that night, God came to me in a short but penetrating dream. In the dream, I stood before a giant Bunsen burner that appeared to be burning brightly beneath a large copper bowl. The flame was powerful, heating up the copper bowl, which began to glow as a carpet of fire covered its base. As I continued to watch, my standpoint changed so that I could now see over the lip of the bowl. Inside the bowl, I could see a liquid bubbling away furiously. The frothy, seething liquid appeared to be a mixture of pure gold and a dark sludge that was clearly some kind of impurity in the gold. I lifted my eyes as I caught a sudden movement above me, and observed a large hand holding what looked like a child's fishing net. The hand swooped down, plunging the net into the boiling liquid and scooping up a fair portion of the vile sludge that lay at the top. As the gunk was lifted out, more of the pure gold could be seen, which now shimmered and glistened.

In the morning, I knew right away that God had spoken to me in another dream, so I asked him for an interpretation and forgiveness for raging at him the night before. The upshot of what he conveyed to my heart was that restoration was a journey, not a quick fix. To help me understand my destination, however, God had given me a taste of his inexpressible peace (Phil. 4:7). While the anxiety had undeniably returned, I was never again to experience another debilitating panic attack. In the presence of God, something unpleasant in my heart had been brought to the surface and permanently removed. What I realise now looking back, is that God was revealing something crucial to me about his nature and presence.

On the back of this revelation about himself, he was also showing me how to relate to him, along with the restorative consequences of spending time in his company. His fatherly heart yearns to see the souls of his children rid of impurities like fear and anxiety. Moreover, I had prayed to God for direction, and realised that he was lighting up the path ahead of me using a simple but profound dream.

There are four key aspects to the dream of purified gold that I want to explore here:

- *The blazing fire* — the glorious presence of the living God
- *The copper bowl* — earthen vessels inhabited by an exceptional God
- *Turning up the heat* — honest prayers and heartfelt worship to God
- *Gold refined in fire* — the perfect God who restores imperfect people.

In the reflections that follow, we will see that there is an extraordinary God who delights in relating to, living in and working through ordinary people (James 5:17).

Turning Up the Heat

The Presence of the Lord

Ever had breakfast with a man who came back from the grave? Strange or absurd as this question might seem, Peter and the other disciples did exactly that (see John 21). In his resurrected form, shortly after being raised from the dead, Jesus passed through material walls (John 20:19), yet presented himself tangibly to witnesses (John 20:27), before eating fish for breakfast on a beach with his disciples (John 21:10-14).

He was raised from the dead by his heavenly Father, because it was impossible for death to keep hold of him (Acts 2:24). His enduring presence still touches millions of lives today, offering unparalleled hope. He is the unending *I am*, destined to come back and save those who have put their trust in him (Heb. 9:28). This is why authentic Christianity is at heart a relationship rather than a religion (John 17:3), and why Jesus announced that those who hear his voice will live (John 5:25). Dead people do not speak; only the living and present are capable of doing that (John 8:58).

The Father too is an undying presence who longs to make himself known to his people (Heb. 1:1-2). Our sins once stood as a barrier to knowing him, but now he has made a way for us to access him through the blood of his Son (Heb. 10:19-22). The incalculably high price of gaining this access ought to signify how vital the Lord's presence is.

One episode during the Israelites' exodus, after God led them out of Egypt, highlights the centrality of God's presence. God commanded Moses to lead the people of Israel and take possession of a land flowing with milk and honey, but stipulated that he would not personally accompany them (Exo. 33:1-3). His refusal to grace the Israelites with his presence was due to fierce anger that he held against them for worshipping false idols (see Exodus 32). Distressed by the looming prospect of God withdrawing from their midst, the Israelites threw themselves into deep mourning (Exo. 33:4-6). Meanwhile, Moses sought to make restitution on Israel's behalf, entering the *tent of meeting* where he spoke to God as one friend might speak to another (Exo. 33:7-11).

In his subsequent exchange with God, it is clear that Moses viewed the prospect of the Lord disengaging from Israel as an unmitigated disaster. As such, he pleaded for reinstatement of the divine presence by reminding God of his personal commitments to Israel and Moses himself (Exo. 33:12-13). This bold strategy elicited a favourable response from the Lord, causing him to relent and make a pledge to Moses that he would now accompany him, and by extension escort the people of Israel as well (Exo. 33:14). In turn, Moses acknowledged the primacy of the Lord's presence, expressing a truth that remains as vital today as then:

> *"How will anyone know that you are pleased with me and with your people unless you go with us? What else will distinguish me and your people from all the other people on the face of the earth?"*
>
> Exo. 33:16, NIVUK

In light of Moses' confession, I believe that the Lord's presence is critical to restoration. When individuals or churches lose sight of the centrality of God's presence, elevating other priorities above pursuit of the Lord's glorious and revitalising company, we rob ourselves and others of the possibility of the extraordinary.

Every major breakthrough in my life has involved a transformative encounter with the Lord, whether in my bedroom or in a congregation; and every setback in my life, of which there have been many, has involved turning my back on the Lord or engaging in formulaic behaviour, which is a substitute for genuine faith in God. (I am including myself in the problem here, so please bear with me.) My heart longs to see the fire of God's presence erupting in hearts up and down the face of Scotland, and to see signs and wonders restored as normative experience, and not just as mere curiosity or a sideshow, mostly kept out of public view. I want to see the sick healed by God on an unprecedented scale, impossible to keep hidden. The key to all of this is to erect 'tents of meeting' up and down the land, in churches, homes and other gathering places, with hungry hearts pressing in to encounter God.

Two thousand years ago, a group of about a hundred and twenty believers gathered in an upper room in Jerusalem following the resurrection of Jesus and his ascension to heaven. Jesus had earlier told them to wait for the power of the Holy Spirit to come upon them, to enable them to be his witnesses to the ends of the earth (Acts 1:8). This reaching across the face of the earth was to be done entirely in God's strength, for his glory and his alone. When the Spirit fell on the assembled believers, a loud wind could be heard in the room, and what resembled tongues of fire rested on each person who spoke in another tongue as enabled by the Spirit (Acts 2:1-4). This fire was the presence and power of Almighty God, a force so strong and vital that it could not be contained in a solitary room or amidst a single group of people, instead rushing out like a divine hurricane into the streets. In one unusual day marked by extraordinary sights and sounds, around three thousand people were added to the new-born church (Acts 2:41). *Come, Lord, and pour out into the streets once again!*

Heavenly Treasure in Earthen Vessels

Have you ever considered where you would live if money was no object? Perhaps you are perfectly happy where you are, or perhaps you dream of sunnier climes and exotic surroundings. On this topic, I am unquestionably conservative, preferring somewhere safe to live and close to essential amenities.

Reflections of a Broken Son

Functional and yawn-inducing perhaps, but I cautioned you before about that quieter side to my nature. Perhaps I need to unleash the inner adventurer more often and let him rip up convention, but I suspect that he would relocate close to savanna grasslands where majestic lions roam and hunt down their prey. (In my mind's eye, I can see my wife and children cheerfully waving me off at the airport as I venture forth to embrace this exciting new life.)

When we pray to our Father in heaven (Matt. 6:9), we are acknowledging that heaven is the dwelling place of the Most High. Heaven is his definitive home, a fact attested on several occasions by Jesus (Matt. 23:9; Mark 11:25); but that is only one part of the picture. His presence is unbounded and fills the heavens and the earth (Jer. 23:23-24), with more than enough presence to make additional homes for himself in human hearts (John 14:23). This is why Paul, using the metaphor of a building to describe believers in Christ, refers to this edifice as a dwelling in which God lives by his Spirit (Eph. 2:22).

While high walls and electrified fences present no barrier to a God who is spirit (John 4:24), finding passage into hard hearts is a trickier though not impossible proposition. By way of illustration, God somehow found passage into the stony heart of Saul of Tarsus, a persecutor of the church of Jesus Christ (Gal. 1:13), who later became known as the Apostle Paul and spiritual father to many of God's people (Gal. 4:19). In light of Saul's astonishing U-turn (as recorded in Acts 9:1-19), consider this: if a man who was instrumental in acts of violence against the church can be saved, then God can make his home in any person, even the chief of sinners (1 Tim. 1:15).

God showed mercy to Paul because he had acted in ignorance prior to his conversion (1 Tim. 1:13). All of this is to say, that God is not looking to take up residence in dream homes with unspoiled features: the Spirit of the Lord will occupy any contrite heart, regardless of history or condition, bringing about spiritual awakening and wholeness (Jer. 24:7; Ezek. 11:19). He is the ultimate home renovator, restoring hope to us and pouring out his love into our hearts (Rom. 5:5).

As believers, the degree to which we appreciate that the sovereign God lives in us, and the degree of reverence that we hold in accordance with that revelation, is related to our maturity in Christ. In his correspondence with the Christians at Corinth, Paul wrote that he was shocked to hear reports about sexual immorality of an unusual nature among their ranks (see 1 Corinthians 6 and 2 Corinthians 2 for details). In this context, he exhorts Christians to flee from sexual immorality, pointing out that the physical body of a believer is the temple of the Holy Spirit (1 Cor. 6:18-19). By this, Paul spotlights a firm connection between persistence in immoral behaviour and failure in believers to properly comprehend that they are the earthly dwelling place of the Most High. The antidote to this ignorance is to ask for and receive greater wisdom from God (Eph. 1:17), and awaken more fully to our identity in Christ as God's own children (Eph. 1:5).

To better grasp the immensity of the revelation that God lives in ordinary people, it should be recognised that he considers living in our hearts to be a massive upgrade to living in a tabernacle (tent of worship) or a stone temple. In the Old Testament, his visible presence (*Shekinah Glory*) was housed in the tabernacle within a curtained-off area known as the Most Holy Place (details of this can be found in the books of Exodus and Leviticus). Later in Israel's history, God's manifest presence took up residence in a beautiful stone temple built by decree of King Solomon (1 Kings 8:1-11). By means of this transition, housing arrangements for God's visible presence were raised to a higher level. You would think that God might settle for the resplendent setting of an ornate temple, but he had an even more prized destination in mind for his sovereign presence: the hearts of common people (Ezek. 36:27; Rom.

8:11). This was always the vision burning in the heart of Father God: we are the end-point of his quest to find a home. We are the earthen vessels into which he has deposited a great heavenly treasure for his glory:

> *But we have this treasure in jars of clay to show that this all-surpassing power is from God and not from us.*
>
> 2 Cor. 4:7, NIVUK

Soothing Aromas to God

A short while after my experience of God's peace in the church sanctuary and asking God for direction, I found myself unemployed for the first and only time in my life. As months rolled by, I became increasingly restless and began to cry out to God for productive employment. One morning during that time, a recruitment advertisement for an agency working with homeless people was brought to my attention. Later that day, I sat under a tree on a grassy embankment at the top of John Street in Glasgow to get some shade and respite from a hot summer sun. As I leaned against the tree and closed my eyes, I began to pray as follows:

> *Lord, I have been alive for thirty years now and have never heard of this agency, and I could probably go for as long without ever hearing about it again. If it is part of your will that I join this agency, then please send me someone today who will speak to me about the agency without me first having to speak its name. If you do that, then I will sign up.*

After ten minutes, I got up and strode back down the hilly street. Coming towards me in the opposite direction was a girl I barely knew from church. As she approached, I felt a sudden

Turning Up the Heat

compulsion to ask her where she had been. While she was still about twenty steps away from me, I shouted out to ask her where she had been. In my eagerness to comply with the strong urge rising in my spirit, I must have appeared extremely rude and abrupt, but the question was like a plum stone caught in my throat that urgently needed to be dislodged. The girl winced with surprise at my hastiness, but gave me a civil reply nevertheless, explaining that she had just left a board meeting of the specific agency that I had just finished praying about. I thanked her profusely, before running off at a pace – once again with the rudeness and abruptness – leaving her with a mystified look on her face. (Or was that horror?)

Shortly after this experience, I joined the agency, serving homeless people over the next year in the streets of Glasgow. During this time, I met a homeless man, John, who became a close friend and whom I led to the Lord after explaining my faith to him one day over a cup of tea. I was not in the habit of leading many people to Christ in those days, so this was an unexpected turn of events. Being a man of the streets, John moved on after a number of years and I lost contact with him, but I know that he is in the good hands of the Lord wherever he might be today.

The type of prayer that I have outlined above, along with the one that I mentioned earlier in relation to the Lord's sign given to me to stop fasting, is one that I refer to as a *wool fleece prayer*. This form of prayer, in which confirmation is sought from the Lord to verify his will, takes its name after Gideon's fleece (Judg. 6:33-40). When Gideon was rallying the troops of Israel to face their enemies in combat, he sought assurance from God that he would lead Israel to victory as God had promised him. To obtain this assurance, Gideon laid out a wool fleece on dry ground, then asked God to deposit morning dew on the fleece but leave the ground around the fleece dry. In the morning, Gideon saw a dew-soaked fleece sitting on dry ground, and filled a bowl with the dew squeezed from the fleece.

Reflections of a Broken Son

To make sure that this was not just some amazing coincidence, he asked God to do it again, this time the other way around. The next morning, he awoke to find a bone-dry fleece sitting atop dew-moistened ground. By this unusual means, God gave Gideon the confidence that he needed to lead Israel into battle. In my experience, God will also answer our prayers when we lay out a "fleece" before him, but we need to do this with pure motives (James 4:3).

There are many forms of prayer in addition to wool fleece prayers. I have already mentioned praying in the Spirit (Eph. 6:18). This was the type of prayer that I was engaged in before being consumed by a flood of peace. While the Apostle Paul encourages us to pray in the Spirit, he also encourages us to pray with our minds (1 Cor. 14:15). Indeed, there are too many forms of prayer to adequately cover in this book. My point in discussing prayer is not to promote any specific type, but simply to encourage genuine prayer of any kind, submitting requests to a compassionate God who does not want us to live in worry or lack:

> *Do not be anxious about anything, but in every situation, by prayer and petition, with thanksgiving, present your requests to God.*
> Phil. 4:6, NIVUK

God delights in the prayers of his people (Prov. 15:8), which rise up to heaven as a soothing aroma to him (Rev. 8:3-4).

While different forms of prayer are important, the condition of a heart offering up prayer is vastly more important. The story of Hannah (as told in 1 Samuel 1:1-2:11) drives this point home. Hannah was married to Elkanah, but unable to have a child because the Lord had closed her womb. Within the prevailing culture of the day, this was a source of profound shame to her. To add insult to injury, Elkanah's other wife, Peninah, and mother of his children, saw Hannah's predicament as an opportunity to torment her, frequently reducing Hannah to tears.

Turning Up the Heat

In her misery, Hannah set off with a burning entreaty in her heart to the house of the Lord. There she sought God, giving up her entreaty to him wordlessly and weeping bitterly in full public view. As a result of the urgent cry of her heart for a son, and a promise to dedicate him to the service of God, the Lord opened her womb and she gave birth to Samuel. Her son would subsequently go on to become one of Israel's greatest ever prophets and leaders.

This was not manicured prayer, wrapped in eloquent speech; it was raw and heartfelt. It is my firm conviction that prayers submitted to God with unclothed passion like Hannah's, trigger a forceful response from the Father. When we playact in front of God or other people, crafting our prayers like works of art for display, we will find heaven's door shut (Matt. 6:1-4). God is looking for the unfeigned responses of our hearts. The words that we use are far less important than the postures that we hold within ourselves. If we want to see our prayers answered and not just heard, then we need to check that they are flowing out of circumcised hearts. We need to keep in sight that we have moved from the Old Covenant arrangements based on outward rituals to the New Covenant arrangements based on deeper inward realities. God knows which side of the fence we are on when we open our mouths to pray:

> *People may be right in their own eyes, but the Lord examines their heart.*
>
> Prov. 21:2, NLT

Not only are our honest prayers a soothing aroma to God, but our acts of authentic worship also present a pleasing fragrance to him. There is no stone-tablet prescription concerning what is meant by worship, as Paul testifies:

> *Therefore, I urge you, brothers and sisters, in view of God's mercy, to offer your bodies as a living sacrifice, holy and pleasing to God – this is your true and proper worship.*
>
> Rom. 12:1, NIVUK

Reflections of a Broken Son

In light of Paul's description here, all acts of love and devotion given to the Lord are essentially acts of worship. This includes, but goes far beyond, songs of worship. Moreover, these acts are to be conducted in Spirit and truth, because those are the type of worshippers that the Father seeks (John 4:23-24). By this, we can see once again that God's spotlight is on inward realities and not on outward performance; so that should be our emphasis too, lest we end up offering hollow sounds and vain tributes to heaven.

One New Testament story shines a light on the nature of true worship. In the story of Jesus anointed with perfume by a woman of ill-repute (Luke 7:36-50), we see what pure worship looks like. In brief, a religious man, Simon, was hosting a dinner party for Jesus, along with some other guests. In this setting, a local woman of disrepute stepped up to Jesus. Defying social etiquette, she threw herself at his feet, washing them in tears and kissing them. Then, breaking open an alabaster jar, she anointed his feet with costly perfume. These acts of adoration moved the heart of Jesus to forgive her for her sins. Meanwhile, Simon and his guests took umbrage at Jesus for what they regarded as folly and impiety on his part for interacting with a 'sinner'. Aware of Simon's disapproval, Jesus chided him for not offering him the common courtesies of the day, including washing his feet, kissing him and anointing his head with oil, all of which the woman had given to him in alternative, worshipful forms. The humble and passionate heart of the woman had touched the heart of Jesus, releasing his blessing of forgiveness, while Simon's fault-finding attitude had deprived him of the blessing.

As I have reflected on this story, this woman's heartfelt act of worship has served as a diagnostic X-ray, essentially laying bare my own acts of worship. If even a fraction of my devotions to God carried the weight of this woman's passion, I would be more than half way up the Lord's mountain (Ps. 24:3-4).

Turning Up the Heat

Recently, I felt the Lord challenging me to consider Jesus' words on the necessity of pouring new wine into new rather than old wineskins (Matt. 9:17). The context in which this challenge arose was my firm belief that a new wine of God's refreshing is about to be poured out over the face of the earth, heralding the return of Christ (Acts 3:19-21). I sense that my old wineskin approaches to worship will not be enough in the coming days. Our hearts are alabaster jars which, breaking open in unadorned worship, will release a scent of costly perfume upwards to heaven; and, in light of this, I sense that it is time for me to turn up the heat and discover new ways of worshipping God.

When Imperfect Meets Perfect

A few months ago, I was preparing to give a talk on the woman with an issue of blood who received healing from Christ. I was working up some notes based on the account written by Luke (see Luke 8:43-48). As I read the account several times, using a biblical commentary to assist my understanding and praying in the Spirit for insight, I had a moment of clarity concerning God's dealings with imperfect people, a revelation that turned my thinking upside down and uncovered some rigid views that I had been holding within myself. While this revelation still continues to unfold in my heart and my understanding remains incomplete, I feel emboldened to share my imperfect contemplations here on the subject of human imperfection. (That is a whole heap of imperfection in one sentence right there.)

In short, the story tells of a woman with constant bleeding who had exhausted herself and her finances over a twelve year period in pursuit of a cure. Over that time, no doctor had been able to provide her with a remedy. Then she got wind of Jesus coming to town. She had likely heard reports of his extraordinary healings from friends, neighbours or relatives. With a large crowd pressing all around Jesus, she moved towards him with one driving objective: *If I touch the hem of this man's garment, I will be healed.* In the eyes of Jewish society at that time, this woman's actions were high-risk, in that her condition made her a pariah, ceremonially and socially unclean. Moreover, the wisdom of the day would have instilled in her a view that her 'uncleanness' could be transmitted to others by touch, like a contagious disease. Thus, an attempt on her part to touch someone in public was culturally taboo and precarious in terms of her own personal wellbeing, especially if caught.

Ploughing through the huddled masses, the woman approached Jesus stealthily from behind in the hope of not being noticed. On reaching him, she crouched low and caught one of the tassels dangling at the bottom of Jesus' outer garment. In that moment of connection, power flowed out of Jesus, entering the woman's body and instantly stemming the issue of blood. Sensing that power had left his person, Jesus demanded to know who had touched him, much to the incredulity of his disciples who thought his question absurd in face of the seething tide of humanity all around him. When the woman realised what had happened to her, she fell to her knees in front of Jesus and explained to all within earshot her reason for touching him and told them what had happened to her on making contact. After listening to what the woman had to say, Jesus confirmed to her and everyone else present, that it was her faith that had made her well.

On reflection, a couple of points have deeply impressed themselves on me concerning the nature of this healing. First, this woman did not follow any conventions of healing, such as the laying on of hands (Luke 4:40; Acts 28:8). She had no desire to have Jesus lay his hands on her, because she was almost certainly hostage to the customary belief that her so-called uncleanness could be transferred onto other people through skin-to-skin contact. Her faith was thus likely mixed with cultural superstition, suggesting that she sought God for healing

Turning Up the Heat

with an imperfect understanding. She nevertheless possessed a roaring fire of faith in her heart that drove her to make unorthodox contact with the one person whom she knew could heal her.

The upshot of her faith and determination to be healed was a miraculous end to twelve years of physical and emotional torment. So, here is what turned my thinking upside down: simply put, the woman's mixed broth of faith and superstition did not prevent divine healing from happening. Despite her imperfect outlook and idiosyncratic strategy to obtain healing from God, her faith was sufficient to open heaven's floodgates, drawing power out of Jesus, even in the absence of forethought or active consent on his part. This does not mean that she stole a blessing from God; her healing was simply a magnificent convergence between her spirited faith in the Lord and his readiness and ability to heal those who seek him out.

The second point that captivated me on reading this story, was that many people in the crowd would have unintentionally brushed up against Jesus in all of the jostling, while others would have consciously stretched out their hands to touch him with all of the fascination and adulation typically reserved for a modern-day celebrity. Yet none of those multiple contacts, accidental or deliberate, drew power out of Jesus. Only the nervous woman possessing dogged faith in her God, and daring to step outside of social convention, triggered that specific outcome. It strikes me that the underdogs and dark horses of society, those less bound to the herd instinct and driven by a strong urge to encounter God, press on to receive the blessing. Jesus knew the difference between a casual touch to his person, and one marked by yearning for real engagement. Jesus does not want us simply to brush up against him, instead being eager for us to make purposeful connection with him; and in that place of unfeigned intimacy, his power is graciously released.

Reflections of a Broken Son

As I have pondered these things, I have had a few unconscious illusions shattered, including that we need to adhere to perfectly accurate doctrine on healing or possess pure faith before God heals us. The bleeding woman's ideas were a blend of fallacy and faith. God did not wait for this woman to get her act together, attend a theological seminary and resolve her defective ideas before he healed her. He met her at her point of need, with all of her flaws and misconceptions, because he saw the bright flame of genuine faith burning in her imperfect heart.

Looking back at my own life, I realise that despite my theological deficits at any given point in time, God has dealt kindly and powerfully with me on many occasions, without requirement to sit an examination on spiritual matters. This does not mean that we should not pursue growth in our understanding, only to say that we will never have complete spiritual insight in this present life (1 Cor. 13:12). My dream of gold being purified in the fire means that there will always be impurities in our nature to be removed, including faulty thinking. Here is the good news: we do not have to wait until some mythical graduation day to receive a blessing from God. The Father sees past the imperfections of his children (Eph. 1:4), blessing them lavishly (Eph. 1:3), and changing their hearts through the interventions and nurture of his Spirit (1 Sam. 10:9; 2 Cor. 3:18).

Chapter 8

Coming Out From the Trees

When God speaks, what he says will come to pass (Ezek. 12:25). It is simply impossible for him to renege on his promises. From the moment that God promised to restore my life over thirty years ago, it was a done deal. Since that time, I have experienced a persistent series of tremors from heaven, rippling out from the heart of Father God and progressively breaking me loose from deep bondages in my heart. While these welcome tremors have enhanced my life in an unhurried and incremental fashion, I was unprepared for the earth-shaking tremor that God unleashed into my life in August 2018. All that I have written up to this point, has been to lay down a scriptural context for recounting this experience, establishing that God does not intervene in our lives with groundless cause. Everything is worked out by the Father in the lives of his children for their good (Rom. 8:28) and his promises to us in Christ are guaranteed (Eph. 1:11-14), even when they seem to be a long time coming (2 Pet. 3:9).

In the remaining narrative of this chapter, I will describe a series of events culminating in the personal earthquake that I have alluded to. For the purpose of presentation, I will detail these events as discrete dots in a larger puzzle, much in the manner that I experienced them at the time of their occurrence, and ask readers to exercise some patience. I will connect the dots at the end of this chapter in line with the pattern shown to me by the Holy Spirit in October 2018, when he opened my eyes to see the path that I had been travelling on, brought by God to a place of profound inner release.

The Prisoner

One of my favourite television programmes of all time is a late 1960s production, *The Prisoner,* starring Patrick McGoohan. It was unique in its day, and its wilful quirkiness has ensured that it remains unique even today and a cult favourite. Prominent among its themes is the conflict arising between societal conformity and individual freedom. In brief, McGoohan plays a recently resigned intelligence agent who is abducted and deposited against his will into a Kafkaesque society known as The Village, sealed off from the outside world and ruled with an iron fist by forces unknown. In this nightmarish setting, the dehumanising designation of Number Six is allotted to McGoohan's character by his captors, who seek to break his will at every turn and extract from him his reasons for resigning from his job. Every week, as an eight-year old child, I rooted for the charismatic Number Six, a feisty rebel armed only with caustic sarcasm and two mean fists. I am grateful to my parents for allowing me to watch this outlandish, drug-addled piece of television, though I sense it was more an act of sufferance on their part as they waited patiently to watch the next episode of *The Forsyte Saga*, or some other grown-up fare of no interest to me.

In chapter 2, I offered some insight into my struggle with anxiety. I want to expand on this just a little more, to show the extent to which I was a prisoner inside myself. The root of my problem was a deep-seated fear of other people's opinions of me. The merest hint of disapproval, by word or gesture, presented a terror to me like no other. This fear was like a vicious claw wrapped tightly around my heart, and some days it was so bad that it felt like calculated torture.

Every day, from my late twenties to early forties, I hid this side of myself, putting on a face while petrified that my fig-leaf mask would slip. Each time, however, the fight to conceal my fears would prove to be futile, and I would end up lacking the strength and wherewithal to extinguish the inferno of anxiety within myself. This was my dream of the worn-out superhero coming to pass, as I repeatedly rose up and crashed to the ground, exhausted and defeated. At those times, I became so ill that I needed time off work to be away from other people, with the exception of family and close friends. The last time I was off work was six years ago, in 2014, so this has not been some short-lived struggle; it has stretched over most of my adult life, peaking in my early forties and gradually diminishing thereafter with God's help. At the lowest points of that difficult journey, I just wanted to be dead and at peace.

In truth, I was bound by a crippling sense of rejection. Looking back, I can see that over-thinking and over-sensitivity were the unhelpful caretakers that fed this beast, giving it life and form. I had created a perfect Frankenstein creature within myself, in the secret gothic laboratory of my inner self, with long ugly bolts driven deep into my heart. (Boris Karloff would have been impressed.) I was stuck in a labyrinthine nightmare of my own making. Unlike the prison of The Village, however, my own incarceration was intangible and not something that I could punch my way out of with McGoohan panache. I derive no shame in confessing that I needed help; and I rejoice in professing that help was at hand.

The Helping Hand

In 2002, after twenty years of limping along with anxiety, I finally went to my doctor for help. I could say that I came to my senses, but the truth is that my wife Lesley, on noticing a disturbing decline in my mood after three years of marriage, robustly ordered – erm, kindly suggested – that I get medical help, convinced that I was suffering from anxiety and depression. My wife has always been an emotionally intelligent person, but the emergency klaxon level of anxiety that I was projecting at that time would have required her to be emotionally tone-deaf to a worrying degree.

The moment that I sought professional help for my problems was a major turning point in my life. After scoring 22 out of 23 on an anxiety and depression scale of some nature – the perfectionist in me has always regretted that shortfall of one mark – the doctor put me on appropriate medication and a suitable path of recovery. Part of my recovery was cognitive behavioural therapy (CBT), which proved to be a life-saver. CBT offered me a lighthouse steering me away from rocks of self-defeating scenarios endlessly played out in my mind.

In view of these interventions, which I regard as a God-send, I am a champion of Christians taking medication and undertaking therapies for mental health problems when necessary. I have no truck with unsafe, super-spiritual nonsense that regards the use of pills as a sign of weakness or faithlessness. Would prescribing spectacles for less than 20:20 vision be held in such contempt? (If you suffer from anxiety and are reading this book, and a Job's comforter in your church has insisted that you ditch your tablets, get professional advice instead. If your doctor agrees with this course of action, then you will likely be advised on coming off your medication gradually rather than stopping abruptly. God is not stupid, so we should not occupy a world of stupid either.)

Coming Out From the Trees

Another critical part of my recovery was counselling. Two different counsellors, Gwen and Ian, gave me perspectives and insights that I would never have formed without their support. These two amazing and highly gifted individuals were both seasoned Christian counsellors. While there are various forms of counselling available to people, Christian counselling offered me two benefits as a believer in Christ: first, a counsellor who can relate to struggles of faith from an empathetic rather than merely sympathetic standpoint; and second, biblical input – I am a firm believer that the word of Christ is charged with life and able to set us free (John 6:63, 8:32).

The above steps were critical building blocks in the process of my recovery, just as the Law of Moses was a critical step towards the salvation of the human race; and while the law was only a provisional measure in the salvation story, in a similar vein, something deeper than medication, CBT and counselling (even Christian counselling) was required for my full inward recovery. Three years ago, and fifteen years after first seeking professional help for anxiety, Jesus began to open up a number of truths in my heart towards a life-changing encounter with him, one that would grant me mental and emotional release on a scale that I had never experienced before.

The first of three critical, and on reflection preparatory, revelations came the day after I had completed the two-day inner healing course in September 2017 (as described earlier in chapter 6). My wife and I both recognised that something had been lifted off our hearts through the actions of forgiving, dealing with past hurts and addressing unbeliefs.

On the morning after finishing the course, I lay in a bath pondering the truths that had been opened up to me over the previous two days and praying in the Spirit. As I prayed, the Father spoke to my heart: *It's time for you to come out from the trees, son.* This interjection, by now a well-established feature of my prayer times, stopped me in my tracks as I waited on the

Reflections of a Broken Son

Lord for more understanding. Quickly, I recognised the expression as relating to God's call on Adam and Eve to come out from their hiding places in the trees, where they had been trembling with fear on the back of sins committed against God (Gen. 3:8). God did not want them stuck for the rest of their days in condemnation and isolation. As such, his compassionate heart led him to draw Adam and Eve out of hiding, and more importantly to eliminate their fears according to his loving and restorative ways. God was now signalling to me that my time of being stuck 'in the trees' was coming to a close, and that he was about to provide a way out that I could never have conceived of beforehand.

The second revelation came in June 2018, when I attended a dance show featuring my daughter, Emma. At the local village theatre, I watched the young people as they danced to thumping beats, swirling and flickering under flashing lights, as I almost passed out. (*Only kidding, Emma! But not really.*) After the show, we made our way to the car park, where a freakish incident occurred. Emma accidentally dropped her mobile phone down a dry drain, passing through an iron grid with slits so narrow that my fingers could not squeeze through them. As I pondered this later, her phone would have needed to fall in a flawlessly vertical posture, like a perfect-ten scoring, Olympic high diver, and additionally seek out the narrow opening with the precision of Hubert Van Innis, the most decorated archer in Olympic history. That is what I mean by freakish.

For a long time, my wife Lesley, Emma and I stared forlornly through the bolted-down grid, swapping brilliant but futile suggestions with each other. It was about a three-foot drop to the bottom of the drain, where the phone now glinted playfully and mockingly in the streetlight. After running out of ideas, we phoned a couple of friends, Ian and Janice, whose daughter Alannah had also taken part in the show earlier that evening. Ian

Coming Out From the Trees

was an infinitely more useful person than myself in these situations, possessing levels of practicality far beyond my reach.

On arrival, Ian produced a long metal device known as a helping hand, replete with lever and grip. Our initial joy was short-lived, however, when we realised that we could raise the fugitive phone to the underbelly of the grid, but only at a 90-degree angle relative to the narrow opening. With no prospect of fingers getting through the opening, never mind swivelling the phone around to the correct angle for exiting, we all sat on the ground and shared despondency in the spirit of true friendship.

After at least another fifteen minutes had passed, Ian's true genius suddenly kicked into overdrive as he spotted that the torch we had been using to illuminate the drain had a string loop at the end of the handle. Now, raising the phone to the grid, and deploying a combination of impressive brainpower and deft manipulation of the torch string around the phone, Ian managed to poke the top of the phone through the slit. Seeing my one chance, I retrieved the phone in a rapid pincer movement, based loosely on one of General Montgomery's tactics deployed in the Second World War. This was my one meaningful contribution to the rescue mission, allowing me to steal Ian's glory in future retellings of the incident. (I have decided to come clean in this book, however, for the sake of friendship.) Needless to say, the outcome was one happy child and two relieved parents.

Back at home, I placed my head on the pillow thanking God for good friends and the retrieval of my daughter's phone. In that moment, God spoke to my heart. The gist of what was conveyed to me was that the Spirit living in me was my true helping hand (John 14:16-17,26). Moreover, God impressed on me that there was no problem within my heart so deeply entrenched that the Lord's helping hand would be unable to infiltrate the cavernous drain of my troubled emotions and pull it out, including the one great fear that I kept hidden from other people. On that hopeful note, I closed my eyes and entered a fit state of rest that night: the Lord's rest.

Around this same time, I had a third crucial revelation to complete preparations for what was shortly to come. I was studying the book of Genesis, closely examining the life of Abraham and other giants of faith who lived prior to Israel's exodus from Egypt.

One day, I was reading about the birth of twin boys, Perez and Zerah, sons of Tamar and Judah (see Genesis 38 for the circumstances surrounding Tamar becoming pregnant and the subsequent delivery of the twins). In the story of the birthing (Gen 38:27-30), Perez (meaning *breach* or *breakthrough*) and Zerah (meaning *rising* or *dawn*) were in the process of emerging into the world. Seeing the hand of Zerah emerge first, the attending midwife quickly fastened a scarlet thread around his wrist to signify that he was about to become the firstborn, a supremely important status in the culture of that time. However, as Zerah pulled back, Perez, living up to his name, made a break for it, breaching into the light of day in front of Zerah to attain firstborn status and defy the midwife's expectations.

As I read about the birth of the twins, the Holy Spirit would not let me move on to the next chapter of Genesis. Caught in a curious loop, I read the passage about four or five times, until the penny finally dropped that the Spirit wanted to speak to my heart. As I called on him for understanding, he opened up some deeper truths lying within the biblical text (John 16:13-15). (In my experience, the Holy Spirit wants us to deep-dive into God's word and not just skim-read it. The Bible is a reliable roadmap for our lives (2 Tim. 3:16), but we need the indwelling Spirit to fathom some of its deeper truths (Ps. 42:7), especially when seeking to find a modern application to many of the Old Testament events and experiences.)

Coming Out From the Trees

What God spoke to my heart can be summarised as follows (I have added a few appropriate scriptural references as directed by the Lord):

> *Break through, son! [Mic. 2:13] Break out like Perez. Let my Holy Spirit, your helper and spiritual midwife, do the heavy lifting. All I ask of you is that you would 'wriggle' in the Spirit, and with his help press through the obstructions in your life. Push past the old toxic mindsets [Rom. 12:2] and those polluted rivers of self-condemnation. [Rom. 8:1-2] As my child, you are meant for better things in this present world: all is gloriously new in Christ and the old things are passing away. [2 Cor. 5:17] Press on through the darkness and break into the light of my love. [Ps. 56:13; Isa. 9:2]*

This was a powerful revelation to me, especially applicable to all who would desire to leave behind the haunting, condemning voices of their past. Even as Spirit-filled believers, we can still find ourselves tested by entanglements to our past that, with the help of the Spirit, we can face down and overcome. What the revelations of the helping hand and the call to break through conveyed to me, in tandem, was that God is my willing and sovereign helper, but that I too had a role in the process of becoming whole. My job was to 'wriggle' in the Spirit. God was not looking for more striving and bouts of superheroism on my part; only that I would press into his loving presence and breach into the light.

Rats and Claws

The above revelations served as invaluable preambles to a life-changing encounter with Christ in August 2018. On later reflection, I realised that the groundwork for my experience had stretched back more than twenty years. There are two particular divine inputs into my life, going back over that long period of time, which are deeply relevant to a proper understanding of my encounter. So, before outlining the experience itself, I will present two more pieces of the puzzle.

In the mid-1990s, I seriously lost my way morally and spiritually for about three years, despite my strong beliefs in Christ. Unresolved emotional pain had caught up with me, and I began to fall apart once again. As inner turmoil mushroomed and my actions became increasingly erratic, even downright destructive, I attended a Christian counselling service. Over six sessions delivered weekly, a counsellor named Gwen helped me to articulate my pain. During the last session, I was in the middle of describing my crippling sense of rejection when Gwen interrupted me. She explained that she had experienced a vivid dream the previous night, and had not realised what the dream meant until I had laid out my damaged heart in front of her. Now, possessed with clarity, she was certain that God had given her a dream to relay an important message to me.

In the dream, she saw a conference room with a large table. Seated at the table, a group of people were engaged in discussion. At the head of the table, a silhouetted figure sat motionless and silent. The subject of discussion around the table was a giant rat, which Gwen coined as a king rat, lurking in a shadowy corner of the room. Baby rats were popping out of the king rat's body, like pieces of popcorn flaring up in a microwave. (That is how I visualised what Gwen was describing.) In the telling of the dream, Gwen linked the rats to the condition of my heart, inferring that there was some primary and deeply entrenched problem (*king rat*) in my life that was generating a host of secondary problems (*baby rats*).

Meanwhile, the conference attendees were watching the unfolding horror that was my rat-infested dilemma. The first to pipe up and offer a remedy was a preacher, who said, 'He just needs to get the word of God into his system; that will fix the problem.' His preaching efforts came to nothing, however, as the king rat continued to spew out more monstrous progeny.

Next up, a woman with a healing ministry put forward her bright suggestion: 'He just needs someone to lay hands on him and offer up a prayer of healing.' As before, however, failure ensued. This pattern continued along the table, with other well-intentioned folk throwing in their tuppence worth. Despite their best ideas, no solution could be found. When all seemed hopeless, the mysterious figure at the end of the table leaned into view. It was the Lord Jesus. Standing up, he addressed the assembly: 'What he really needs is my touch.' Then, walking over to the king rat, he touched it. At a single touch, the king rat convulsed and died, shrivelling away to nothing. The baby rats that had been feeding off their king also curled up and died, now disconnected from their life-source. The direct touch of Jesus had accomplished what nothing else on earth had been able to do.

After this highly detailed dream was communicated to me, I was left with a strong sense of hope that never left me. I was unclear, however, as to the precise nature of the rats, particularly the king rat, and the exact manner of the dream's fulfilment. Moreover, I was still on a severe downward spiral at that time, which meant that the dream was relegated to the back burner as, once again, chaos closed around me.

Many years after hearing about Gwen's dream of the king rat, I was on a relative upward curve, picking up the pieces of my life and fighting for my emotional health with the help of a second Christian counsellor, Ian. During our last session together, we shut our eyes in closing prayer. As we prayed, God gave Ian a picture in his spirit that he relayed to me. In the picture, he had seen a fierce looking claw with razor-sharp talons clutching my heart. Four gnarled fingers were pressed deep into the underside of my heart, while the thumb of the claw pierced my heart on the topside. As Ian watched, the hand of the Lord appeared and, in a decisive move, the thumb of the claw was forcibly snapped by God. With the thumb rendered useless, the fingers positioned under the heart could no longer find leverage to keep holding on to my heart. The claw, now rendered inoperable, fell away, releasing my heart from bondage.

It was only after Jesus revealed himself in a powerful way to me two years ago, that I realised that Gwen's dream and Ian's picture had been conveying the same truth to me. (I will get to that later.) The various road signs granted to me over a considerable period of time were now about to converge in one remarkable encounter.

Deep Encounter

Recalling the dream of gold refined in the fire (as described in the previous chapter), the contaminants in the gold had to be brought to the surface before being removed. The Lord's presence is both a refining fire (Zech. 13:9; Prov. 17:3) and a river of refreshing (Jer. 31:25; Rev. 22:17), but the bad stuff in our hearts, particularly shame and fear, need to be brought to the surface and removed, before being replaced with the good stuff of the Lord (Isa. 61:7; Gal. 5:22-23). In August 2018, a rapid succession of events brought my deepest shame and its army of attendant fears to the surface, prepping me for a deep encounter with the Lord and profound inner release.

In early August, I was attending a charity event in Glasgow. The event, open to the general public, aimed to distribute a thousand free school bags to children living in poverty. The event was extremely well attended, with hundreds of families present. A personal highlight of the day was seeing the happy faces of children who inadvisedly let me graffiti their faces with face paint. After my third masked superhero effort, I cut loose in the spirit of Salvador Dali, venturing into uncharted places of abstraction. The girls found this approach more endearing than

Coming Out From the Trees

the boys, who reminded me that superheroes were not to be messed with, as I masked up another budding crusader sporting a 'don't give me that abstract garbage' expression.

While enjoying much of the experience, my strong feelings of rejection had flared up. Interacting with a crowd of strangers over a prolonged period of time had stirred a leviathan of pain skulking within my heart. This had left me feeling exhausted, though not to the extent of robbing me of good memories or a sense of satisfaction in taking part in a good cause.

As I sought to catch my breath over the next few days and recuperate from my revived anxieties, I realised that Lesley and I had committed to supporting our church youth leaders by running one of the youth sessions during the summer break. This was to happen on the next Sunday. With rising panic, I envisaged a man spontaneously combusting in front of a horde of youth. Wishing to avoid a fire hazard, I approached my wife to cancel our commitment to leading the youth session. I thought briefly of arguing that it had been *her* commitment rather than *ours*, but self-preservation pulled me back from the brink of a cliff called *Don't Go There!* When I asked my wife for a reprieve, hoping that her wifely kindness would break forth, she stiffened visibly and reminded me that the commitment was binding. I understood the logic of her stance, but was too devastated in that moment to cherish her many outstanding qualities.

Needless to say, a youthful swarm descended on me that Sunday. Manically bouncing off unseen walls inside myself, I led a series of games and quizzes along with my wife. With equal mania, some of the noisier kids broke the sound barrier, with one boy mysteriously upending a table like some magician from the wrong side of the street. In the end, it was good fun; nothing so boisterous as to be over the limit. On the back of the previous weekend's struggles, however, I found myself once

Reflections of a Broken Son

again grappling with irrational fears, up against faceless phantoms and no ejector-seat button to hand.

With fear now well and truly roiling at the surface, I faced a third and final challenge the following weekend. I was due to attend an annual church-based event, an opportunity for men to come together over three days for Christian fellowship and games at a centre in a rural area a few miles outside of Glasgow. Though wearied by my internal struggles, I resisted bowing out of the weekend trip, knowing that God would move powerfully in hearts and that the games on Saturday afternoon would be the usual blast of good fun.

On the Friday evening, the visiting preacher, a man deeply anointed by God, opened up the weekend's proceedings with the story of Elijah hiding in a cave at Horeb due to the murderous threats of Jezebel, after he had run through her prophets with the sword (see 1 Kings 19:1-18 for details).

Seeking a modern application to the Old Testament story (one without swords), the speaker challenged his listeners to consider what 'caves' they found themselves stuck in, and to incline their hearts to God for his gentle whispers to help them out of their places of restriction (1 Kings 19:12-13). Calling men in the room to stand up and allow the Spirit to minister to them, I stood and became enfolded in the Lord's presence as I confessed to being stuck in caves of anxiety, rejection and low self-esteem. For the next while, I basked in great peace, as I sensed God moving in the room and breathing gently on my heart. Though this was not a time of breakthrough, it was nevertheless a moment of deep tranquillity, as God led me in the Spirit to lush pastures and still waters (Ps. 23:2).

On Saturday morning, after breakfast and banter, we assembled again for the second teaching session. This time the speaker spoke about Jesus experiencing complete vulnerability in the Garden of Gethsemane (Luke 22:39-46). There, he drank from the cup of suffering, consuming the dregs of our iniquities and absorbing them fully into himself. In so doing, he embraced the pain of taking his next steps towards death on the cross without the comforting presence of his Father, having only ever experienced uninterrupted intimacy with him up until this moment. Driven by a boundless love for us, Jesus took on the anguish and penalty of forsakenness, which had been due to us for our sins. In his eyes, we were worth the suffering. After this teaching, there was ministry as before, with the peace of the Lord once again enfolding me.

By lunchtime, however, I had reached saturation point in terms of being around other people, even among friends, as hitherto manageable feelings of rejection now bubbled away furiously at the surface. I was hard pressed against the wall of my inner cave, unable to find a way out. Feeling horribly shut in, I made a sudden dash for freedom, chasing after one of the men returning back home that afternoon. Outside, I watched his car speed away into the distance, as I quietly cursed his fleetness.

In frantic search of Plan B, I cried out to God for help. Immediately, the name of a good friend, James, dropped into my heart. He has the capacity to see potential in people that others, even themselves, can sometimes fail to see. On finding James, we retired to a private place to pray. There I opened up the sluice gates of my heart, releasing a tidal wave of anguish. At the end of our time praying together, James got me to stand up and, in a symbolic act of receiving freedom from the Lord, he asked me to enact coming out of my inner cave. Punching the air in front of me to symbolise spiritual breakthrough (*Perez*), I stepped across an imaginary line on the floor representing the edge of my cave, happy to co-operate with God in this unusual and somewhat prophetic manner.

Thanking James for his support, I went outside to be alone with God and my thoughts. Walking around a deserted football pitch, I began to open up my heart to the Lord. Sobbing uninhibitedly,

Reflections of a Broken Son

I released my pain up to heaven. As I discharged wave after convulsive wave of bottled-up shame and fear, heaven responded by discharging wave after glorious wave of inexpressible peace. Under a waterfall of divine refreshing, I sensed emotional sewage being swept away as heaven's crystal-clear waters rushed in (Isa. 44:3).

While more was yet to come, this extraordinary touch from God gave me sufficient strength and lightness of heart to take part in the games that afternoon. As usual, the games were a highlight of the weekend, offering a blend of physical and mental challenges, a flurry of one-liners, wanton laughter and novel ways of cheating (for which there was a virtual trophy of shame). As I took part in the happy proceedings, I was quietly grateful to God for his faithfulness and helping me out of my cave.

The next morning, I awoke still feeling refreshed. As my two roommates headed for breakfast, I chose to stay behind and pray. Giving up a flood of thanksgiving to God and praying in the Spirit, I expressed my gratitude to him. About half an hour into this passionate appreciation of God, I felt the Spirit steering me gently to a place of quietness and stillness. With my eyes closed and hands raised upwards, revelations from the Lord broke out in my heart.

In my mind's eye, I watched Jesus drinking from the cup of suffering. As forsakenness and anguish consumed him, drops of blood-stained sweat poured out of his face and fell to the ground (Luke 22:44). (I do not consider this to have been a metaphor used by the gospel writer, Luke: the more straightforward interpretation is that real blood was actually shed in the Garden of Gethsemane. *Hematidrosis* is a rare condition in which a person in a state of anguish or distress sweats blood. In fact, Leonardo Da Vinci has recorded evidence of soldiers sweating blood before battle.) This was the start of the Lord shedding his

Coming Out From the Trees

blood for humanity and going to war with the spiritual forces of evil holding us captive.

As I considered this, I heard the Spirit whisper to me that the release of blood in the sweat of Jesus was the first public sign of imminent reconciliation between Father God and sinners. Recalling that there is no forgiveness of sins without the shedding of blood (Heb. 9:22), I could see in my spirit that the droplets of blood in the garden were the first visible indication of the Lord's impending acceptance of humanity, made fully available to us after the sacrificial death of Jesus.

As the Lord continued to pour life-affirming truth into my heart, I perceived that Jesus, in his forsakenness, had absorbed our orphanness – that is, our estrangement from the Father – entirely into himself, so that we in turn could be accepted as God's children and made whole by his sacrifice:

> *Surely he took up our pain*
> * and bore our suffering,*
> *yet we considered him punished by God,*
> * stricken by him, and afflicted.*
> *But he was pierced for our transgressions,*
> * he was crushed for our iniquities;*
> *the punishment that brought us peace was on*
> *him, and by his wounds we are healed.*
>   Isa. 53:4-5, NIVUK

This is why Jesus' promise not to leave his disciples in this world as orphans stands good for all time (John 14:18). In the act of becoming separated from the presence of his heavenly Father, from Gethsemane to Calvary and even into the very bowels of the earth itself (Matt. 12:40), Jesus drew the identity of the spiritual orphan into himself, making it possible for us to take on the identity of sons and daughters of God (Isa. 8:18; 2 Cor. 6:18).

As I stood still, drinking this in, I heard the Spirit of God proclaiming an explicit truth in my spirit, over and over: *Jesus' forsakenness is your acceptance.* This truth reverberated in my heart, until I could hear nothing else but the beautiful sound of the Lord's voice and his soothing word of acceptance – no longer a truth solely written in the pages of the Bible, but one imprinted directly onto my heart (Jer. 31:33-34) – washing over every part of my insides and sweeping away boulders of rejection and spiritual orphanness in its wake.

While this powerful revelation has not brought an end to all anxiety in my life, it killed any lingering doubts that I had of being on the outs with my heavenly Father. The revelation of his personal acceptance of me was an epic shifting, from head to heart, of the inviolable truth of the Father's acceptance of all who put their faith in his Son, Jesus Christ (Col. 1:21-22). Since that time, almost two years ago, nothing has budged my deep-rooted sense of belonging to the Father, knowing with the assurances of his indwelling Spirit that I am his son (Gal. 4:6), and through the finished redemptive work of Christ on the cross, that my ultimate destination is heaven not hell (John 14:2-3; Phil. 3:20-21).

The Final Unveiling

Having tasted real freedom in Christ far beyond the mere principle of freedom (John 8:32; Gal. 5:1), I found myself praying one day as follows: *Lord, in a vast sea of possibilities, direct me to the specific books and teaching resources that will open up my eyes to see more of you.* Then something unprecedented happened. God is my witness that, in a short space of weeks, five Christian books were given to me at church, spontaneously and without prompting, by five different friends and acquaintances. I do not recall even one person giving me a single book in this unsolicited fashion prior to my prayer, never mind laying hold of five books in quick succession by different people.

Like a starving man cut loose at an all-you-can-eat buffet, I devoured uplifting truths in quick time, including: living according to the First Commandment (loving God with everything in us; Luke 10:27); enjoying creative ways to worship God; the nature of radical Christian discipleship; living the abundant life through God's grace and keys to entering his rest; and finally, the true meaning of sonship and what it means to be a child of God. This last book was particularly pivotal to the Lord clarifying key aspects of my deep encounter with him.

One day in October 2018, I set off for my usual lunchtime prayer walk in the hospital grounds where I work, enjoying the peaceful stroll along a path winding up a small hill and through a wooded area. As I thanked and praised God for the breakthrough two months previously, I sensed the Spirit moving in me and talking to my heart. He spoke of the long journey that I had been on and granted me a bird's-eye view of the road that had led to my deep encounter with the Lord, and the implications of that encounter. This is fundamentally what he conveyed to me:

> *Do you realise that Gwen's dream of the rats and Ian's picture of the claw were expressing the same truth about the nature of your confinement? The king rat and thumb of the claw both represent the same major stronghold – dominant source of oppression – that has hindered you for most of your adult life, and the baby rats and fingers of the claw both represent offshoots of the main stronghold. I have been trying to get through your defences for a long time now, but self-protection has prevented you from discerning the truth more swiftly than you have. I have been with you on this long journey, and at*

Reflections of a Broken Son

the point when your heart was sufficiently open to the truth, the Lord Jesus touched the king rat (snapped the thumb of the claw) and broke the stronghold that has hemmed you in for so long. This has brought you to a place of greater freedom – spiritually, mentally and emotionally. Now that you have tasted freedom, you will walk in even greater levels of freedom in the days ahead as you keep your eyes focused on the Lord your God.

I was stunned at the clarity washing over my heart. Moreover, I was taken aback at the depths of my long-term stubbornness and mulish ways. Most of all, however, I was blown away by the vast mercy and unfathomable love of a God who had neither thrown me onto a scrapheap marked *beyond repair*, nor ever left my side (Ps. 94:14; Heb. 13:5). I have been the Father's son right from the moment I called on Jesus more than three decades ago, but I was only now waking up and stepping into a fuller appropriation of that truth.

As I pondered all of this, I asked God to explain the rats and the claw. Using the claw as my guide, I asked God what the four fingers represented, before asking him what the thumb stood for. (Looking back, I wonder if I unconsciously kept the thumb aside for the big reveal, like an Agatha Christie novel where the murderer is not revealed until the last scene.)

In a heartbeat, I sensed the Spirit reveal to me the identity of three of the four fingers: anxiety, depression and low self-esteem. When the identity of the fourth finger did not become apparent right away, I pushed the Lord for an answer. A minute later, as I stepped into the wooded part of my journey, the word *loneliness* jumped into my heart. As a married man with three children and many good friends, I was momentarily confused by this response. Then I sensed the Holy Spirit ask me a question: *You know that feeling when you're in a crowded room*

Coming Out From the Trees

and you feel utterly alone despite the company of others? This question found an echo in my heart, and I knew what God had meant by loneliness. My four persistent accosters – anxiety, depression, low self-esteem and loneliness – had unquestionably left deep scars on the inside over a large part of my life. Yet, what had given them such leverage to thrive in my heart and trample my inner world? What was the thumb that had given these warped fingers the leverage to penetrate so deeply and intrusively into my soul?

Tantalisingly, this question would not be answered fully until January 2020. After reading a book on sonship to the Father, I felt directed to purchase more books on that topic to get a broader view across a different number of authors. Reading about sonship opened my eyes, as if for the first time, to our amazing inheritance in Christ as God's children. As this reality was dawning on me, the Lord dropped the last part of the puzzle into place concerning the thumb of the claw that had been wrapped around my heart for so long. The following effectively captures what I sensed God conveying to my heart during a prayer time four months ago:

> *The thumb of the claw has been your pervasive sense of spiritual orphanness, riddling your heart with feelings of rejection and a continual sense of being on the outside (feeling abandoned). This is the legacy of the Fall worked out in an individual human heart. This is evidence of a life weaned for too long on the fruit of the Tree of Knowledge, drunk on wisdom that opens eyes to see good and evil, yet leaves a man staggering under the weight of himself – the burden of self on the throne. Come now, ditch the lies and fully switch over to the Tree of Life – my beloved Son, Jesus Christ. [John 6:35, 14:6] Actively put on the clothes of my acceptance and put my promise*

Reflections of a Broken Son

ring, the family ring, on your finger, son – you are mine forever! [Luke 15:22] I promised not to leave you as an orphan in this world, [John 14:18] and now you are invited to the banqueting table. So, let the celebrations begin! [Luke 15:23]

These revelations have turned my world upside down. My heart feels like the proverbial tortoise catching up with the frantic hare that is my mind. Scriptures that were once cold truth, now burn like hot coals in a heart that has been deep-frozen for too long. In spiritual terms, I consider myself a toddler who has suddenly realised with utter clarity who his Father is, like a little boy finding his voice for the first time and starting to cry out *'Daddy!'* with real conviction (Gal. 4:6). Even now, I can see in my mind's eye my heavenly Father embracing his son and speaking to me in loving terms: *Well, son, that was a long time coming. Welcome home!*

Chapter 9

The Path of Sonship

One day, while still under lockdown conditions during the coronavirus pandemic, I went for a daily walk with my son David and dog Dudley. Approaching a crossroads in a path, I suddenly noticed a wooden canopy draped across the top of an entrance to a tunnel into which a stream was flowing. I commented to David that I had never noticed this feature before, even after fifteen years of regularly walking past it. (Yes, the pandemic has driven me to this level of banality. I am slowly losing the plot as I run out of topics of conversation with my family, and myself for that matter.)

This incident put me in mind of the story in which Abraham cast out Hagar and Ishmael (Abraham's son by Hagar), expelling them from the family home at the behest of Sarah (Gen. 21:8-21). After running out of water in the desert, Hagar lay her son under a bush and moved a short distance away, unwilling to watch her son die. As she and her child both sobbed, the angel of God called out from heaven and told Hagar not to be afraid, proclaiming to her that God had plans to make Ishmael and his descendants into a mighty nation. Then God opened Hagar's eyes to see a well of water that had escaped her notice up until then, allowing her and her son to drink and be refreshed. The two of them went on to live in the Desert of Paran, where Ishmael grew up and married an Egyptian woman.

Notice that God did not conjure up a well for Hagar; he opened her eyes to see what was already there in front of her. This principle of God opening eyes is pervasive in the Scriptures. Time and again, Jesus miraculously opened the eyes of the physically blind (Luke 4:18). However, he also came into this world to deal with the spiritually blind (John 9:39). An example of Jesus opening spiritually blind eyes is found in the story of Christ walking to Emmaus with two of his followers after his resurrection (Luke 24:13-34). On joining them, Jesus asked them what they were discussing. Not recognising Jesus in his resurrected form, they spoke of the crucifixion of Jesus, the disappearance of his body from the tomb, and their disappointment that he had not delivered Israel from Roman occupation as they had hoped for. Reproachful at their lack of faith, Jesus unlocked hidden truths nestled in the Scriptures, showing them that the Messiah had always been destined to come into the world and suffer before entering his glory. Then, breaking bread with his two companions, their eyes were suddenly opened and they recognised Jesus; that is to say, the Lord caused them to become aware of who was already standing right in front of them.

In this chapter, I want to talk about Jesus opening my eyes to see the path of sonship more clearly. While I have now been a son to the Father in my spirit for over three decades, awakening to that truth and all of its beautiful ramifications has been a slow process due to wrestling with spiritual blindness over a long period. Like the two travellers on the road to Emmaus, my own lack of faith has often prevented me from seeing truths already in front of me. The following section describes a revelation given to me by the Holy Spirit about a year ago giving me clearer sight of sonship and opening up the way for me to walk more confidently and consciously in that reality.

The Path of Sonship

The Three Paths

One day at home last year, as I was praying in the Spirit and reading scriptures aloud (most likely the book of Ephesians, which I was memorising and studying at the time), I suddenly saw a vivid picture appear in front of me as I stood in my living room. I saw three paths in a countryside setting, stretching out in front of me like three prongs of a trident. The path to the left of centre had the word *Rebellious* floating in large block letters above it, and the path to the right of centre had the word *Religious* hovering over it in the same monolithic font. (Religious, as in rule-based religion or works of the law.) Straight down the centre, and stretching towards blazing sunshine, was a path that had the term *Spirit-led* positioned above it. As I looked at these three paths, I heard the voice of the Lord speak to my heart:

> *I am calling you to set your face like flint and walk as my son down the centre path, the one illuminated by my Spirit. [Ps. 143:10; Rom. 8:14] This is the path of sonship that I have set before you, to walk in the light of my Son, Christ. [Eph. 5:8-9; 1 John 1:7] For your own sake and those close to you, stop falling away to the left and right in patterns of self-destructive rebellion and self-righteous piety. Are you not exhausted by now from your own futile exertions? [Prov. 3:5-6; John 6:63] Live in the fullness of life, and not like some spiritual pauper crouching in the margins and shadows. [Deut. 28:13] Walk in my strength with your head lifted up. [1 Chron. 16:11] Live like a son of mine!*

While reflecting on what I was perceiving in my heart, I felt the Holy Spirit directing me to stop reading the passage that I was on and turn to the parable of the lost son (Luke 15:11-32). This was a story that I had read many times before, but just as the Lord granted Hagar and the two travellers to Emmaus new awareness and insight, respectively, I read the story of the lost son with fresh eyes and was accorded a new understanding of sonship by the Spirit. To convey what was shown to me, I will divide the story of the lost son into three episodes according to the three paths, and the three corresponding themes, that I saw in my front room.

The Rebel

The Lost Son, Episode 1: (This part of the story relates to Luke 15:11-19.) A man had two sons. The younger son was impetuous and prone to self-serving ways. One day, in a fit of impatience, he demanded that his father give him his inheritance. Normally, children would acquire their inheritance at the time of their father's death. By his hasty action, this son therefore treated his father badly and effectively made him a dead man in his eyes. Leaving the family estate with a windfall, the son put distance between himself and his father. In a foreign country, he lived a wild, tempestuous life. His days were a blur of hedonism, pitching along until his wealth dried up and the pleasures turned to rust. Now finding himself in an inhospitable place, in the middle of famine and without money or true friends, the son got a job tending pigs and ended up coveting the very pods that the pigs were eating. Realising the error of his ways, he set his mind to return to his father and offer him a grovelling apology. He felt unworthy to call himself a son and steeled himself to be taken on by his father as a mere hired hand.

Rebellion in the church: Traditionally, the tale of the lost son has been taken as a depiction of someone lost in the world, hitting rock bottom and finding salvation in God's kingdom. However, Jesus did not tell this story to those who had already put their faith in him as if it did not concern them. Remember that Jesus spoke in parables for the benefit of those receptive to the truths contained within them (Matt. 13:10-17). With this in mind, Jesus refers in the parable to *sons* throughout. By this is meant family members and, by inference, insiders to the kingdom; so, there is also room to interpret the story as a cautionary tale for believers to avoid rebelling against their heavenly Father. Adopting this angle, there is ample evidence of rebellion in the early church. For example, see the messages of Christ to the seven churches in the Book of Revelations – in particular, his messages to the churches at Pergamum (Rev. 2:12-17) and Thyatira (Rev. 2:18-29). In this context, Jesus highlights problems of Christians promoting and tolerating sin, idol worship, sexual immorality, and propagation of misleading prophecies and teaching. Even if it is a hard truth to swallow, rebellion in the church of Jesus Christ is also unlikely to be a strictly historical problem, unique to our spiritual predecessors. I believe that the lessons in the tale of the rebellious son remain valid until the return of Christ.

Personal reflection on rebellion: Earlier in this book, I alluded to a dark chapter of my life as a believer when I went off the rails. For a significant period in my thirties, I dived heedlessly into rebellious mode, leaving a trail of destruction in my wake. Full of unresolved emotional pain, I drove my faith into a ditch and headed off like the lost son on a blowout. During this season of my life, I was promiscuous and frequently drunk (once again), also delving briefly into drug use (ecstasy). The cost of living like this was ruinous, torpedoing relationships and self-sabotaging. My mental health also took some hard knocks during this period, with anxiety and depression afforded full reign over every aspect of my daily existence. Unable to forgive myself for hurting other people, I stumbled through those shameful days on a cocktail of self-pity and self-hatred. Eventually, God, in an act of sheer grace, pulled me out of my ditch; but only on admitting to the mess and pain I had caused and turning my heart back to him in sincerity. There have been other briefer pockets of rebellion in my life (I will address one of those in the last section of this chapter), but nothing quite on that epic scale. Though I confess to chaotic episodes in my life as a believer, commonly referred to in church circles as *backsliding*, I also testify to a merciful God who brought me back to my senses and reawakened me to his faithfulness and loving care.

Final thought on rebellion: Finally, it is worth noting that rebellion in human hearts is traceable back to the Tree of Knowledge, representing self-directed lives falling on the side of evil; that is, entanglement in more obvious and visible sin.

The Spirit-led Son

The Lost Son, Episode 2: (This part of the story relates to Luke 15:20-24.) Having squandered all of his inheritance, the lost son headed back home empty-handed and broken-hearted. On his journey, he no doubt imagined the angry face of his father on having to report bankruptcy and extravagant days in a far-off country. As he braced himself for a fierce reprimand, the father spied his son approaching the family home while he was still a considerable distance away. Pulling up the hem of his garment, he ran like the wind down the path, full of love and compassion at the sight of his son. On reuniting, the father threw his arms around his son, embracing him with deep joy. The son, taken aback at this unreserved display of fatherly affection, confessed to sinning against his father and heaven itself, and to feeling unworthy of the title *son*. The father would not hear of it; this was his treasured son, restored back to his presence. On seeing the dishevelled appearance of his son, the father told servants to quickly bring him the finest robe in the house, along with a family ring for his finger and sandals for his feet. With gladness of heart, the father also instructed the servants to prepare a feast for his son, with no skimping on festivities. This was to be a happy occasion for a life recovered, not a requiem for days frittered away in a distant land.

The Path of Sonship

The Spirit at work in the church: In light of the above story, the evidence of a Spirit-filled church, is one brimming with lives restored to God, marked by his ownership and authority (fingers adorned with the family ring), and the air characterised by an enriching fragrance of celebration. This is neither revelry nor frivolity; it is a steadfast attitude and expression of thankfulness towards a loving Father who has received us back to his heavenly estate (Eph. 2:19; Phil. 3:20), embracing us through the restorative work of Jesus Christ. The hallmark of Spirit-led Christianity is deep inward joy that will inevitably find an outlet:

> *Every day they continued to meet together in the temple courts. They broke bread in their homes and ate together with glad and sincere hearts, praising God and enjoying the favour of all the people. And the Lord added to their number daily those who were being saved.*
>
> Acts 2:46-47, NIVUK

Too much solemnity in the house of God may be evidence of an orphan culture that, like the lost son, grovels in the face of past mistakes, blocking the flow of grace and sonship. We are to rejoice in the fact that the Lord is not counting our sins against us (Rom. 4:6-8; 2 Cor. 5:17-19) and is calling us to his banqueting table (Song 2:4; Luke 13:29).

Personal reflection on being Spirit-led: A major part of walking with God over three decades has been, with the help of the Spirit, to shed hindrances to knowing him. The more I see him clearly, the stronger the sense of inner peace (*shalom*) has become. A big forward movement in my life was learning to forgive others. During counselling many years ago, anger was identified as a formidable wall built around my heart, a dam of self-protection stemming the flow of God's grace towards me and keeping me bound in depression. Led by the Spirit, I confessed my grievances and resentments before the Lord, releasing forgiveness towards those who had caused me pain. This was a vital step forward into a deeper level of freedom and sonship. Hard as it may sometimes be to forgive others who hurt us, it is indispensable towards becoming more like Christ. Sonship is therefore a path of high calling, demanding that we show mercy to others in the light of God's mercy shown to us (Matt. 6:12, 18:21-35).

Final thought on being Spirit-led: The Apostle Paul defines the children of God as those who are led by the Spirit of God (Rom. 8:14). These are those who learn to wean themselves off the Tree of Knowledge, stepping out of the confines of a self-directed life that spurns God's intimacies, and reconnecting to the Tree of Life – that is, to Christ, our eternal life-source (John 1:1-5) and life-enriching vine (John 15:1-5).

The Rule Keeper

The Lost Son, Episode 3: (This part of the story relates to Luke 15:25-32.) Now, the son who had misspent his inheritance had an older brother, a very different man not prone to indiscipline or unruly passions. He was incessantly busy, dutiful and always about his father's business. Day in and day out, this son attended to tasks around the estate, ensuring that his father's property was kept in good order. On the day of his younger brother's return, the older brother was toiling in the fields as usual, when the unmistakeable sounds of music and dancing began drifting out of the house. A servant told him that a party was in full swing for his brother who had returned home safe and sound. Standing outside the house, the older brother became enraged as he listened to the sounds of good cheer within. The father went outside to invite his son to join the party, but the son was in no mood to celebrate as he lit into his father, rhyming off his credentials as a good son – loyal, decent, hard-working and respectful of the rules. He voiced his disgust at the younger son receiving preferential treatment after tearing up the rules and

The Path of Sonship

living recklessly in a far-off land. The father told his disgruntled son that, far from missing out, the family property was still his birthright; lock, stock and barrel. He also reminded his son that his younger brother had effectively come back from the dead, and that his homecoming was therefore cause for much celebration.

Rule keeping in the church: Restoration in Jesus Christ is achieved through inward transformation (circumcision) of the heart by the Holy Spirit (Rom. 8:2), and not through external rule keeping (Acts 13:39). Reliance on ritualistic patterns of behaviour for salvation is sometimes referred to as *legalism* (in other words, works of the law). The heart that pulls away from being led by the Spirit (the mark of authentic sonship), falling into legalism instead, will find no spiritual life to draw on. Like the older son in the story of the lost son, legalism can stultify the heart and make us critical of those who deviate from our set of rules. Jesus warns us of this kind of arrogance in his parable of the Good Samaritan (Luke 10:25-37), where he makes it abundantly clear that he is looking for good-heartedness and not religious rule keeping.

As was the case with rebellion, there is plenty of evidence of legalism in the early church. For example, the Christians in Galatia forsook the promise of the Holy Spirit, instead opting for conformity to a set of rituals tied to specific dates in the calendar (Gal. 4:8-11). Other examples include: the church at Ephesus, where passion for God and his kingdom was lost in pursuit of correctness and intolerance of charlatanism (Rev. 2:1-7); the church at Sardis, where a reputation for looking good and being spiritually alive masked a spiritual deadness (Rev. 3:1-6); and the church at Laodicea, where arrogance blinded them to their spiritual poverty (Rev. 3:14-21). Moreover, these examples are provided in the Bible to warn us that these problems can still exist in the church today.

Reflections of a Broken Son

Personal reflection on rule keeping: One of the greatest tricks that Satan deploys to hamstring our spiritual development is to convince us that spiritual impediments and shortcomings, including legalism, are always someone else's problem – never ours! Yet, here is a thought: why then did Jesus have to tell his innermost circle of disciples to beware *'the yeast of the Pharisees and Sadducees'*? (Matt. 16:5-12) – that is, to avoid the pitfall of trying to be saved by our own pious efforts. In fact, the Apostle Peter would proceed to fall into that very trap for a short period of time, until the Apostle Paul confronted him and reminded him that only faith in Jesus Christ puts us right with God (see Galatians 2 for details).

Looking back, I can see several moments in my walk with God where I lost sight of my Father's love and fell into patterns of self-righteous piety. In fact, my epic descent into rebellion, as described above, was preceded by a two-year period of legalism, a time when my faith was put on the back burner and replaced with religious posturing. I was treading fallow ground, finding no real spiritual sustenance, and I firmly believe that this was a classic case of pride preceding a fall. Rule keeping has never changed my heart in a long walk with God; only glimpses of a love too great for me to fully comprehend has ever brought me to my senses and set my feet on a right path.

Final thought on rule keeping: Attempts to gain favour and salvation from God through rule keeping, rather than by faith in God and his free gift of life in Christ, is traceable back to the Tree of Knowledge, representing self-directed lives falling on the side of 'good'; that is, entanglement in less obvious and invisible sin.

....

The three paths above have been three that I have walked on at various stages of my life since conversion to Christianity. This call of God upon my life to choose the centre path of sonship, led by the Spirit, was conveyed to me because it is always a possibility to veer off onto the other two paths. God will never eliminate our freewill: loving him is a daily, as well as a lifetime, choice. Inevitably, we will make mistakes and God is willing that we get back up quickly, dust ourselves down and proceed on the right track. Before describing a recent situation where I had to do exactly that, I want to explore the interdependent nature between rebellion and rule-keeping forms of religion, given that they both draw from the same source (the Tree of Knowledge).

An Unholy Union

After Adam and Eve were expelled from the Garden of Eden, they gave birth to two sons, Cain and Abel (Genesis 4 has the full account). Cain grew up to become a crop farmer and Abel a tender of livestock. One day, the two men presented their offerings to the Lord. Cain brought fruits of the soil and Abel portions of fat taken from the firstborn of his flock, which he had sacrificed. In due course, God manifestly expressed approval of Abel's offering and disapproval of Cain's. Aware of God's displeasure at his offering, anger flared up in Cain and his face fell. Seeing his dejection, God confronted Cain and told him that if he had done what was right, his offering would have been accepted. Essentially, he had presented God with a bloodless offering, representing the works of his own hands and betraying his lack of faith in God, unlike the straightforward faith of his brother Abel.

Cain now stood at a crossroads: he could stem the flow of sinful impulses prowling around his angry heart or give vent to them. Unwilling to humble himself, he looked around to find release for his incendiary emotions and cast an envious and murderous eye on his brother. One day while they were alone together in a field, Cain killed Abel, staining the soil with his innocent brother's blood. In the face of such terrible injustice, God had no choice but to punish Cain, stripping him of his livelihood and making him a fugitive on earth for the rest of his days. Though deeply angry at Cain, God nonetheless put a mark of divine protection on him to ensure that no-one would take his life, despite the fact that Cain had taken one himself; proving that when sin abounds, God's grace always abounds more (Rom. 5:20).

For a long time, I could only see one side to Cain in this tragic story; namely, that he was humanity's first murderer, a conniving man who savagely killed his own brother. The treachery of Cain is sin at its most flagrant, exemplifying the outflow of evil from humanity's attachment to the Tree of Knowledge. What I failed to appreciate for a long time, however, was that Cain was also a pious man who had dealings with God. He brought offerings to God, conversed with him and understood the value of the Lord's presence (see Gen. 4:3-16). Arrogance and presumption, however, were his downfall and the wellspring to murder. The pride nestled in Cain's heart is sin at its most furtive, exemplifying the outflow of 'good' – or what passes for good to spiritually blind eyes – stemming from the Tree of Knowledge. In the downward spiral of his life, Cain illustrates all aspects of our involvement with the Tree of Knowledge, with rebellion and self-conceit proving to be deadly bedfellows.

This is why many religious leaders were instrumental in the murder of Jesus. Here was a man declaring the good news of God's mercy towards sinners, even forgiving them publicly (Mark 2:5; Luke 7:48), while these 'guardians' of law and order were busy carving a self-accredited path to heaven. Jesus and his revolutionary message of God's grace presented a direct threat to their standing, upending everything that they stood for; and like wild animals backed into a corner, they viciously rounded on him and manipulated the Roman authorities into killing him. By their self-preserving actions, we can see in them the same pernicious marriage of rebellion and self-conceit that blighted Cain. In the final analysis then, the paths of the rebel and rule keeper ultimately converge, both leading human hearts away from God's sovereignty and presence. Like the head and tail of a coin, they are two sides of a single reality: a fallen humanity that denies God and his gift of grace towards us in Jesus Christ.

Rebellion and rule keeping – i.e., the pursuit of rule keeping as a means to salvation – are essentially an unholy union. Indeed, the Apostle Paul reveals a symbiotic relationship between rebellion and legalism (rule keeping) when he writes to the church at Corinth:

> *For sin is the sting that results in death, and the law gives sin its power.*
> 1 Cor. 15:56, NLT

The true meaning of the expression, *the law gives sin its power*, is laid bare in Romans 7, where Paul describes sin as a destructive force that has secreted its way into human nature like a cuckoo that has infiltrated the nest of our hearts (Rom. 7:18-20). Paul explains that the use of law as a means to combat this parasitical force is doomed to failure, because sin, entrenched in our nature, will always find a way to circumvent or even break the rules. In fact, keeping the law is a suppression strategy rather than a cure for sin – in the same way that social distancing is a suppression measure rather than a cure for coronavirus – and such suppression of sin simply allows it to thrive in the heart and become even stronger (Rom. 7:7-12). Hence, Paul's unusual statement that the law gives sin its power, and also an explanation for why certain religious people in Jesus' day were able to do abominable and hateful things to Jesus.

Paul then goes on to assert that there is only one way to truly destroy sin: redemption in Christ and deep cleansing of our nature through God's life-giving Spirit (Rom. 8:1-2). We find freedom from the tyranny of sin only by the enlivening and transformative presence of the Holy Spirit within us (Rom. 8:9-11). Our own feeble efforts to abide by the rules will inevitably capsize (Rom. 3:20; Gal. 3:10-11). This is why Paul constantly reminds us that our salvation rests squarely on the sacrifice of Jesus and not on law keeping (Rom. 3:23-28). In the matter of our salvation, taking our eyes off Christ and his finished work of redemption on the cross, and forsaking the promise of the Spirit who is given to guide and purify us, only ever produces failure (Gal. 3:1-4).

The Father's Heart

In closing this chapter, I want to express the most significant thing that I can say about Spirit-led sonship: we cannot enter into the full freedom and reality of sonship until we know the true heart of our heavenly Father. Over and over in public discourse, Jesus underlined the centrality of possessing an authentic knowledge of the Father:

> *Then Jesus, still teaching in the temple courts, cried out, 'Yes, you know me, and you know where I am from. I am not here on my own authority, but he who sent me is true. You do not know him, but I know him because I am from him and he sent me.'*
>
> John 7:28-29, NIVUK

Jesus' intimate knowledge of his Father defined him and set him apart in every possible way, colouring and suffusing his identity, his character, his public ministry and his mission on earth to rescue us. Until we too know the Father with clear-sightedness, we may continue to limp along with orphaned

The Path of Sonship

sensibilities, striving to please God like employees or hired servants (John 15:15), rather than enjoying and demonstrating the fruits of being his children (Matt. 7:16-20).

Last year, the Father kicked down some unhelpful walls in my heart, giving me a life-changing glimpse of his generosity that radically altered my view of his nature. It was a moment of clarity concerning his love, releasing me into a greater understanding and experience of his kindness.

In March 2019, my wife and I attended a one-day Christian conference in Stirling, along with relatives and friends. During an extraordinary day of anointed biblical teaching and powerful ministry, a couple with strong prophetic giftings were busy working the room throughout the day, delivering words of hope and encouragement to attendees in a personal way. In the afternoon, the husband stepped over to Lesley and I and, with our permission, proceeded to pour out uplifting words over us. I offer here an extract of what was relayed to us (recorded on my phone at the time):

> *I saw the Lord pulling up these big rigs [spotlights] for you, like those on a construction site, and they are illuminating the whole highway for you…So, it's really a walk now over the next five months where everything just seems very visible…and so decisions are going to be very easy for you to make. But then I see that it's like the lights are going to begin to dim and you are going to have to remember that, 'I [the Lord] was with you when it was all illuminated, and I am still with you as the lights begin to go down.' I see a time when everything goes really dark, but inside you is the light you've already been carrying. And this is the reason that I see you going through a doorway – popping through a door is how I would put it – because there's been*

other people struggling to get anywhere. And what you are doing is that you are passing that light onto them, illuminating them so that they can begin to see their pathway. So, what is really a huge discovery right now is that you have weathered the storm; you're going into the light, and now you're going to pass that same thing on to others.

Here is what happened after these words were spoken: from April to August 2019, during the five-month period following the prophetic message above, intimacy with God came easily on a daily basis. Personal prayer and worship times felt rich and effortless, and revelations from God, many of which appear in this chapter, were like streams of light passing unhindered from God's own heart to my own. Then, at some point in August, I remembered the word about everything going really dark after five months. Being prone to rumination, I began fretting about this unspecified darkness. In the absence of a name, I went into overdrive and began filling in the blanks in my troubled mind: bereavement (my top suspect); sickness (less threatening but still a worry); my wife walking out on me (hold on, she's seen the worst of me – relax!); me walking out on my wife (no chance! – she's a keeper); and a score of other undesirables vying for my attention. When I confessed this smorgasbord of misery to my wife, she laughed in my face, kindly to the last, and said something along these lines: 'Really!? Is that how your mind works? I haven't given it much thought since it was spoken. If it comes to pass, then God's in charge. Give yourself a break!'

Like a window opened, allowing a fresh breeze to pour into a room full of stagnant air, Lesley's straight-speaking blew away the worst of my fears. So, with thoughts of disaster put to bed, I ventured serenely into September only to be ambushed by darkness of an unforeseen nature. God is my witness that I had no hand in engineering the following events, and it was only later, once events had passed and the lights came back on, that I realised what had happened. (Light has a way of doing that.)

One morning, I woke up in a shockingly foul mood. It appeared to spring out of nowhere and was all-encompassing. In a fit of pique, I shut God out and switched off the lights. I refused to pray or listen out for his voice, read the Scriptures or spend any time in his company. I blanked him like the huffiest man on earth; or, as my kids would say, I 'patched' him. For the next ten days, I was unreachable, lurching around with an out-of-office sign hung around my heart.

On the eleventh day, I awoke to discover a deeply unsettling wave of anxiety forcing its way up to the surface of my heart. This was the tipping point. That evening, I sat with Lesley and confessed to my strange and unreasoning neglect of God – a churlish sabbatical, if you will. At the same time, she confessed to struggles with starting a new college course on counselling. ('Why be miserable alone' is my selfish motto.) Taking the bull by the horns, we both prayed and gave up our respective cares to God; and in my own case, an apology for being dismissive towards the Lord.

The next day at work, and the twelfth day after emotional lockdown, I found myself praying enthusiastically at lunch time. A door had popped open in my heart, and spiritual truths came flooding in like bright lights filling a gloomy room that had been boarded up for eleven days. The Father spoke to me of his perfect love and my need to embrace that love (1 John 4:7-12; Eph. 5:1-2). He further spoke of his love in all of its glorious, undiluted reality – not my filtered or limited interpretations of it – being the only currency that will convince a bruised humanity of his kindly intentions towards all people (Rom. 5:5-8). Moreover, when the Lord is known in a wholehearted way and his love is clearly reflected in his children, his renown will go forth and cover the face of the earth (Ps. 46:10; John 17:20-23).

On the way back home, I became overwhelmed with joy as I realised that my Father had dealt with me in an undeservedly generous way. I had spurned him, turning off the lights with no fault on his part. On giving up my foolish neglect of God, he in turn had embraced me without hesitation like the father who ran to hug his rebellious son on the homeward path, lavishing me with love and understanding. To make sense of how big-hearted the Lord had been towards me, I pictured myself snubbing Lesley solidly for eleven days. In my mind's eye, I saw a blood-chilling frostiness cross her otherwise lovely features, and a frightened man sent to the doghouse for a substantial season. To help me comprehend his gracious attitude, the Lord broke it down for me as I worshipped him on my drive home, revealing truths to me along the following lines:

> *At the moment of my Son's death on the cross, the curtain standing in front of the Most Holy Place within the temple was torn from top to bottom, [Matt. 27:51] signifying that the way back into my holy presence was now opened up by his sacrifice. [Heb. 10:19-22] The door to my fatherly heart therefore never shuts, son; but when you embarked on your own self-imposed blackout, you shut the door on your side, not mine. My love towards you never wavers. I saw you standing in a bad mood on the porch outside my house, like the older son in the parable of the lost son. The estate is still yours, and your inheritance is still intact. However, the feast is prepared, and it would be good if you ditched the self-defeating attitudes and came in for the party. Take my advice, son: dive into and remain in the ocean of my fathomless love. [Rom. 8:37-39]*

The Path of Sonship

This revelation has irreversibly altered my view of God. I feel like a son with cataracts removed, now seeing my heavenly Father with a clarity that excites me to my core. This is not the stern God of fussy, hard-nosed religion. This is a merciful God who works patiently in the hearts of his children to awaken them to a love that will never end.

> *We don't yet see things clearly. We're squinting in a fog, peering through a mist. But it won't be long before the weather clears and the sun shines bright! We'll see it all then, see it all as clearly as God sees us, knowing him directly just as he knows us! But for right now, until that completeness, we have three things to do to lead us toward that consummation: Trust steadily in God, hope unswervingly, love extravagantly. And the best of the three is love.*
>
> 1 Cor. 13:12-13, MSG

Reflections of a Broken Son

Chapter 10
From Here to Eternity

When I survey the path that I have trod now for over three decades, I marvel at one thing: the steadfast determination of my heavenly Father to fulfil his promises. With unswerving resolve and gifted hands, he takes on the projects that others would throw on the scrapheap or would cause them to reach reflexively for the delete button. On my worst days, I have vied with Paul for title of *chief sinner,* but I will settle for *twenty-first century fool with weather-beaten insides and torn face to match* (less succinct but probably accurate). While I still experience difficult days – steer clear when you see the glum signs – there is an unshakeable love, joy and peace growing quietly inside me. I am pregnant with sonship, and my spiritual belly keeps swelling as time goes on. (My wife will tell you that the pandemic crisis has had a similar effect on my physical constitution – her relentless honesty is my reality-check, as well as my inspiration.)

Meanwhile, I look around at the helter-skelter world that I live in, bustling with people clamouring to be heard and pushing furiously for their rights to be elevated to the top of the world's in-tray. Responsibility and respect, it would seem, have quietly resigned and may now be found drinking pina coladas on a distant tropical beach, paving the way for a sinister new culture of self-promotion and creeping intolerance.

Over two thousand years ago, one man inaugurated a counter-culture kingdom, one that dares to put others first. He ushered in this kingdom by letting cruel hands drive nails through his own merciful, outstretched hands. Imagine, then, a world propelled by selfless love for others, rather than one increasingly haunted by division and injustice. The fact that some immature believers and outright impostors have done appalling things in the name of Jesus Christ does not detract from the truthfulness of his words, the exquisiteness of his unsullied heart and his unrivalled power to restore our lives (Eph. 1:18-21). The Spirit of Christ is a spirit of deep love and a cure for angry, restless hearts. I also believe that the Father's love is the lifeline available to us in a world that appears to be slipping into chaos.

I realise that by writing this book that I am just one more voice in a swirling sea of competing voices, but I have no cause célèbre to offer – only a story about a God who has loved me for no other reason that I can fathom than that it is fundamentally his nature to love, and to do so in an uncommon fashion. It has taken me decades to begin to appreciate his goodness in a proper way, leaving me increasingly awestruck and more inclined to love him right back – that is, to love him from the heart rather than dutifully or unquestioningly. I am wonderfully ruined for him the longer I proceed on this journey. I would also love to offer readers an immaculate conclusion in this closing chapter, but I am mid-journey, half-formed and still indecently rough around the edges. Sonship is a lengthy process and happens inwardly by the renewing power of the Spirit and our co-operation, one degree at a time (2 Cor. 3:18).

I set out to write this book with two key sets of people uppermost in my mind: those disaffected by formal religion and those struggling with anxiety who wonder if God could ever truly free them up. I have not walked a conventional walk with God, so my hat goes off to those who feel similarly displaced, kicked out of Conformity Town (a variation of The Village). The God I have come to know was not a conformist either, spurning an easy life of convention for a barbaric instrument of torture, a wooden cross; and all in the name of love. If you feel like an outsider, then do not worry. Paul, one of the greatest ever followers of Christ, while revered today at a safe distance long after his death, was treated like garbage by many people while he still drew breath:

> *It seems to me that God has put us who bear his Message on stage in a theatre in which no one wants to buy a ticket. We're something everyone stands around and stares at, like an accident in the street. We're the Messiah's misfits. You might be sure of yourselves, but we live in the midst of frailties and uncertainties. You might be well-thought-of by others, but we're mostly kicked around. Much of the time we don't have enough to eat, we wear patched and threadbare clothes, we get doors slammed in our faces, and we pick up odd jobs anywhere we can to eke out a living. When they call us names, we say, 'God bless you.' When they spread rumours about us, we put in a good word for them. We're treated like garbage, potato peelings from the culture's kitchen. And it's not getting any better.*
>
> 1 Cor. 4:9-13, MSG

It is easy to revere someone once they are gone, when we can sterilise their teachings and remould them to suit our own religious narratives. I am certain in my own heart, however, that Paul would be as inconvenient in society today as he was when he walked the earth, at least to those who have diluted or rejected his uncompromising message of God's gift of grace

Reflections of a Broken Son

towards us in Jesus Christ (Rom. 3:20-24, 4:13-17). This is good news for those who know with all of their heart that they could never earn such extravagant love by their own merits. They know too much about themselves to pretend otherwise; and perhaps have a long parade of witnesses to further corroborate that self-perception.

As for the question of whether or not God can break our mental and emotional shackles, only I truly know the radical changes that have occurred within my bruised soul; though my wife will also testify to a better husband today than the one she sent to the doctor's surgery eighteen years ago. I am the Lord's broken son in a broken generation. I still carry internal scars and do not pretend in any way to be fully patched up. Stand at a hundred paces away from me and you will still likely see me limping along with a measure of self-doubt. However, my love for my Father has blossomed and reached a place of effortless reciprocation: he loves me and I love him. It has always been effortless on his side; it's only starting to become that way on my side. He is this to me: my best friend and supporter; my anchor and strength; my protector and everlasting Father.

As I press forwards into greater freedom and security, and eventually to my final resting place with my beloved Father, I fall to my knees in adoration of Jesus who went into heaven before me. He is this to me: my light and wisdom; my rescuer and hero; my Lord and my God (John 20:28). He has taken this lost son and led him back to his heavenly Father's estate. I give further praise to the Spirit who has opened my eyes, and continues to open them wider as he shows me the endless wonders of God's kingdom. He is this to me: my helper and teacher; my comforter and nurturer; my vigour and vitality. He provides the breath necessary to step into the future with confidence.

So, when I look ahead, I see with an optimism that seems a million miles away from the suicidal thoughts that once danced

From Here to Eternity

on the cracks of my heart. I am still that misfit who cried on a bed in Greenock; but I am the Lord's and he is mine. This has been a love story at heart, and the beauty of it is that it is never-ending. I do not know what the future holds – no-one ever truly does – except that the Lord is standing there every step of the way; and the love that he pours out never stops, not even in eternity.

Reflections of a Broken Son

Twelve Questions for Reflection

1. **What do you think it means to know Jesus in a personal way?**

Key scriptures:

> *I am the good shepherd; I know my own sheep, and they know me just as my Father knows me and I know the Father. So I sacrifice my life for the sheep.*
>
> John 10:14-15, NLT

> *Yes, everything else is worthless when compared with the infinite value of knowing Christ Jesus my Lord. For his sake I have discarded everything else, counting it all as garbage, so that I could gain Christ*
>
> Phil. 3:8, NLT

> *May God give you more and more grace and peace as you grow in your knowledge of God and Jesus our Lord.*
>
> 2 Pet. 1:2, NLT

For reflection:
Jesus is waiting for you to let him into your heart. He is ready for you to encounter him in a personal way, no matter the history or present condition of your life. He is humble and will not force himself on you. A walk with him is an adventure of faith. If you want to be reconciled to your heavenly Father, Jesus has made that possible. If you want assurance that you will spend eternity in a place of peace and rest, Jesus provides that guarantee. If you want freed up from mental and emotional pain in this present life, then

Reflections of a Broken Son

there is one who has the power to release you: Jesus Christ. He is a prayer and a heartbeat away.

Your own thoughts or prayer on personally knowing Jesus (write below):

Twelve Questions for Reflection

2. What parts of your life would you consider disqualify you from God's mercy?

Key scriptures:

> *For as high as the heavens are above the earth, so great is his love for those who fear him; as far as the east is from the west, so far has he removed our transgressions from us.*
> Ps. 103:11-12, NIVUK

> *And they will not need to teach their neighbours, nor will they need to teach their relatives, saying, 'You should know the LORD.' For everyone, from the least to the greatest, will know me already. And I will forgive their wickedness, and I will never again remember their sins.*
> Heb. 8:11-12, NLT

> *If we claim that we're free of sin, we're only fooling ourselves. A claim like that is errant nonsense. On the other hand, if we admit our sins—make a clean breast of them—he won't let us down; he'll be true to himself. He'll forgive our sins and purge us of all wrongdoing.*
> 1 John 1:8-9, MSG

For reflection:
God is merciful and longs to enfold us in his love, like the father in the parable of the lost son who ran to embrace his repentant son on his return home. Once our sins are sincerely confessed, they are removed to a distance from the heart of God that is defined as incalculable (*as far as the east is from the west*). As such, the Lord promises that he will never again call to mind those sins. He wipes the slate clean because he has no desire or inclination to hold our sins

Reflections of a Broken Son

against us. We can confess wrongdoing to the Lord, confidently bury our mistakes in his mercy, and take an assured step forward in his love.

Your own thoughts or prayer on the Lord's mercy (write below):

Twelve Questions for Reflection

3. To what extent do you believe that God keeps his promises?

Key scriptures:

> *God is not a man, so he does not lie. He is not human, so he does not change his mind. Has he ever spoken and failed to act? Has he ever promised and not carried it through?*
> Num. 23:19, NLT

> *As you can see, I'm about to go the way we all end up going. Know this with all your heart, with everything in you, that not one detail has failed of all the good things GOD, your God, promised you. It has all happened. Nothing's left undone – not so much as a word.*
> Josh. 23:14, MSG

> *For no matter how many promises God has made, they are 'Yes' in Christ. And so through him the 'Amen' is spoken by us to the glory of God.*
> 2 Cor. 1:20, NIVUK

For reflection:
Are you tired of people breaking their promises? Even loved ones can let us down and leave us hurting in the wake of yet another broken promise. I am aware that many people see God as just another big lie (a religious conspiracy) – or if he does exist, that his promises appear worthless in an often-chaotic world. Yet that is not true. He promised Eve that one of her descendants would come one day and save the human race. That is exactly what happened – no ifs or buts; no defaulting on the contract; guaranteed in precious blood! Jesus Christ is the promised redeemer and restorer who gave

up everything to remove our sins and re-establish relations between ourselves and our heavenly Father. His love overthrows the chaos. God is an uncompromising promise-keeper, right through to the very core of his being.

Your own thoughts or prayer on God as promise-keeper (write below):

Twelve Questions for Reflection

4. What do you think is required to put people right with God?

Key scriptures:

> *Jesus is 'the stone you masons threw out, which is now the cornerstone.' Salvation comes no other way; no other name has been or will be given to us by which we can be saved, only this one.*
>
> Acts 4:11-12, MSG

> *When we were utterly helpless, Christ came at just the right time and died for us sinners. Now, most people would not be willing to die for an upright person, though someone might perhaps be willing to die for a person who is especially good. But God showed his great love for us by sending Christ to die for us while we were still sinners.*
>
> Rom. 5:6-8, NLT

> *But when the kindness and love of God our Saviour appeared, he saved us, not because of righteous things we had done, but because of his mercy. He saved us through the washing of rebirth and renewal by the Holy Spirit.*
>
> Titus 3:4-5, NIVUK

For reflection:
All of the good works under the sun will not put us right with God. We can devote ourselves to goodness all of our days and we will still not be one inch closer to the Father. He sent his only begotten Son to deal with the problem of estrangement between ourselves and himself: sin in our hearts. Faith in Christ is the only remedy for sin and an end

to separation from God, providing mercy and a deep, thorough cleansing of our hearts. We can try to approach God any other way, but only Jesus provides a genuine pathway back into our heavenly Father's presence. Salvation in Christ is a gracious gift from God given to those who are completely incapable of saving themselves – that is, to all peoples on earth.

Your own thoughts or prayer on being put right with God (write below):

Twelve Questions for Reflection

5. What is your purpose in life?

Key scriptures:

> *'For I know the plans I have for you,' says the LORD. 'They are plans for good and not for disaster, to give you a future and a hope.'*
>
> Jer. 29:11, NLT

> *And we know that in all things God works for the good of those who love him, who have been called according to his purpose.*
>
> Rom. 8:28, NIVUK

> *It's in Christ that we find out who we are and what we are living for. Long before we first heard of Christ and got our hopes up, he had his eye on us, had designs on us for glorious living, part of the overall purpose he is working out in everything and everyone.*
>
> Eph. 1:11-12, MSG

For reflection:
Many people find purpose in relationships, family, career, wealth-making, fame, humanitarian causes, and countless other goals and pursuits. These are not bad in themselves, but they fall well short of what God has in mind for us. God is not out to rob us of the good things in life; he wants us to prosper and have the best things in life. The problem arises when we find it hard to believe that God can work things out better for us than we can by our own efforts (even Abraham made this mistake). The Tree of Knowledge sways us to trust our own instincts, live by our own wisdom and protect our own interests (for good or evil). The Tree of Life (Jesus Christ) reconnects us to a far higher and more

fruitful reality. The Lord's purpose for our lives is to free us up to rediscover the intimacies that we enjoyed with him before the Fall. In recovery of this intimacy, we also find renewed purpose in rejecting hatred and loving other people (even our worst critics).

Your own thoughts or prayer on having purpose in life (write below):

Twelve Questions for Reflection

6. When you are stressed, who or what do you turn to for peace and rest?

Key scriptures:

> *The LORD bless you and keep you; the LORD make his face shine on you and be gracious to you; the LORD turn his face towards you and give you peace.*
>
> Num. 6:24-26, NIVUK

> *Are you tired? Worn out? Burned out on religion? Come to me. Get away with me and you'll recover your life. I'll show you how to take a real rest. Walk with me and work with me—watch how I do it. Learn the unforced rhythms of grace. I won't lay anything heavy or ill-fitting on you. Keep company with me and you'll learn to live freely and lightly.*
>
> Matt. 11:28-30, MSG

> *Don't worry about anything; instead, pray about everything. Tell God what you need, and thank him for all he has done. Then you will experience God's peace, which exceeds anything we can understand. His peace will guard your hearts and minds as you live in Christ Jesus.*
>
> Phil. 4:6-7, NLT

For reflection:
The Lord wants us to offload our worries on him. He longs for us to entrust him with our lives, and is more than willing to help us and meet our needs. Continuously fretting and striving in our own strength blocks the flow of God's grace into our hearts and situations. The more we come to know the true gracious nature of the Father, the more we will see

Reflections of a Broken Son

that he is the continual gift-giver who wants us to fully place ourselves in his divinely capable hands. As we learn to rest in him, step by step, his peace will flow into those parts of us that once laboured anxiously to make ends meet. The Lord's rest – a gift to his children – leads to more fruitful living and better results in all areas of our lives, practical and spiritual.

Your own thoughts or prayer on seeking peace and rest (write below):

Twelve Questions for Reflection

7. What does the idea or reality of experiencing God's presence mean to you?

Key scriptures:

> *GOD said, 'My presence will go with you. I'll see the journey to the end.' Moses said, 'If your presence doesn't take the lead here, call this trip off right now. How else will it be known that you're with me in this, with me and your people? Are you traveling with us or not? How else will we know that we're special, I and your people, among all other people on this planet Earth?'*
>
> Exo. 33:14-16, MSG

> *You make known to me the path of life; you will fill me with joy in your presence, with eternal pleasures at your right hand.*
>
> Ps. 16:11, NIVUK

> *Look! I stand at the door and knock. If you hear my voice and open the door, I will come in, and we will share a meal together as friends.*
>
> Rev. 3:20, NLT

For reflection:
The primacy of God's presence flew under the radar of the religious enemies of Jesus and led to them dying in their sins. Due to spiritual blindness, these critics of Jesus elevated compliance over reliance; that is, compliance with rules over reliance on the Lord's renewing presence and his matchless power. Christians can fail to grasp this issue as well. For example, the Galatian Christians started really well, enjoying God's favour and his miracles as the Lord's presence wrought signs and wonders in their midst. Sadly,

they reverted to type, re-embracing religious conventions and abandoning the Lord's presence – that is, trading the promise of the Spirit for a programme of self-perfection. The absence of miracles can be an indication of compliance over reliance; of ritual over renewal; of 'truth' over Jesus (*The Way, the Truth and the Life*).

Your own thoughts or prayer on God's presence (write below):

Twelve Questions for Reflection

8. What level of confidence do you possess that your prayers will be answered?

Key scriptures:

> *GOD's there, listening for all who pray, for all who pray and mean it.*
> Ps. 145:18, MSG

> *Ask and it will be given to you; seek and you will find; knock and the door will be opened to you.*
> Matt. 7:7, NIVUK

> *If you need wisdom, ask our generous God, and he will give it to you. He will not rebuke you for asking. But when you ask him, be sure that your faith is in God alone. Do not waver, for a person with divided loyalty is as unsettled as a wave of the sea that is blown and tossed by the wind.*
> James 1:5-6, NLT

For reflection:
We do not need to be perfect to get answers from God to our prayers. All he is looking for is prayers offered up to him straight from the heart – no cleverness; no bargaining; no hidden motives; pure and simple. I believe that every honest prayer directed to God gets an answer. The answer can be 'Yes', 'No' or 'Wait'. That may sound like a cop-out, and one that gives God license to argue that he has answered our prayers regardless of whether or not we know that he has. In my experience, however, God often answers 'Yes' and exceeds what is asked for. When he answers 'No', I have found that he thoughtfully reveals why the answer is 'No', and has often course-corrected me when my prayers have been marred by impure motives or he had something better

in mind than what was asked for. Finally, when the answer is 'Wait' it is usually issued when there is a vital matter of timing involved that only God in his infinite wisdom can orchestrate. In those cases, the outcome is always more than worth the wait.

Your own thoughts or prayer on having your prayers answered (write below):

Twelve Questions for Reflection

9. Are there ways by which you try to measure up to get a blessing from God? (For example, by praying longer or harder)

Key scriptures:

All praise to God, the Father of our Lord Jesus Christ, who has blessed us with every spiritual blessing in the heavenly realms because we are united with Christ. Even before he made the world, God loved us and chose us in Christ to be holy and without fault in his eyes.
Eph. 1:3-4, NLT

Each time he said, 'My grace is all you need. My power works best in weakness.' So now I am glad to boast about my weaknesses, so that the power of Christ can work through me.
2 Cor. 12:9, NLT

I would like to learn just one thing from you: did you receive the Spirit by the works of the law, or by believing what you heard? Are you so foolish? After beginning by means of the Spirit, are you now trying to finish by means of the flesh?
Gal. 3:2-3, NIVUK

For reflection:
In Christ, Father God accepts us as we are, regarding us as his faultless children. We can breathe a sigh of relief. It's not our imperfections that get in the way of the Lord's blessings, it's our perfectionism (striving to perfect ourselves). God knows our many faults, right down to the last detail, and his answer to our shortcomings is the renewing power of his Spirit (heart circumcision), not our own insufficient self-improvements. He is ready to lavish us

Reflections of a Broken Son

with fatherly love and generosity despite our faults. Don't wait for faultlessness – Jesus alone is sinless – or a big muscular faith before asking the Lord for a blessing. God's glory is magnified in our weakness and reliance on him.

Your own thoughts or prayer on receiving blessings from God (write below):

Twelve Questions for Reflection

10. Is there anything in your heart that you would want mended?

Key scriptures:

> *The LORD is close to the broken-hearted and saves those who are crushed in spirit.*
>
> Ps. 34:18, NIVUK

> *The high and lofty one who lives in eternity, the Holy One, says this: 'I live in the high and holy place with those whose spirits are contrite and humble. I restore the crushed spirit of the humble and revive the courage of those with repentant hearts.'*
>
> Isa. 57:15, NLT

> *I'm leaving you well and whole. That's my parting gift to you. Peace. I don't leave you the way you're used to being left – feeling abandoned, bereft. So don't be upset. Don't be distraught.*
>
> John 14:27, MSG

For reflection:
While God can immediately heal people in physical ways, he can also heal a broken heart, though this is not generally an instant process. God works in us to mend our broken hearts over time. In my experience, he sometimes removes a specific fear in a moment – perhaps through deliverance (e.g., from a stressful situation), an encouraging word or some other divine intervention to uplift us. Concerning more entrenched patterns of shame and fear in our lives, these rooted conditions or habits require deeper cleansing and circumcision of the heart by the Spirit. I am often unaware of what needs to be fixed until the Lord casts light

Reflections of a Broken Son

on hindrances nestled in my heart. However, a walk with God is not always about being fixed up – sometimes we just need to relax in our brokenness, comforted by the peace of the Lord, until his tenacious healing touch restores us again in perfect time.

Your own thoughts or prayer on God healing broken hearts (write below):

Twelve Questions for Reflection

11. What would your life look like if it was completely Spirit-led?

Key scriptures:

> *So don't you see that we don't owe this old do-it-yourself life one red cent. There's nothing in it for us, nothing at all. The best thing to do is give it a decent burial and get on with your new life. God's Spirit beckons. There are things to do and places to go!*
> Rom. 8:12-14, MSG

> *And we all, who with unveiled faces contemplate the Lord's glory, are being transformed into his image with ever-increasing glory, which comes from the Lord, who is the Spirit.*
> 2 Cor. 3:18, NIVUK

> *But the Holy Spirit produces this kind of fruit in our lives: love, joy, peace, patience, kindness, goodness, faithfulness, gentleness, and self-control. There is no law against these things!*
> Gal. 5:22-23, NLT

For reflection:
Jesus promised us the Holy Spirit. The Spirit guides us, comforts us, helps us and, as we open up to him, fills our hearts and restores us to Christ-likeness. A walk in the Spirit is continual reliance on God for what is unattainable through human effort. To the untrained eye, Spirit-led actions can look like human effort, but when a person's actions are propelled by and infused with the Lord's Spirit, the outcome is radically transformed lives: renewed thinking; healing and wholeness; restored relationships; souls added to the

kingdom; sustained spiritual life and growth, etc. The Spirit does nothing but impart and instil life: he replenishes dry wells, revives dry bones and invigorates wearied hearts, resuscitating our hopes and dreams. He issues a river of life that keeps welling up in our hearts over time – *abundant life!*

Your own thoughts or prayer on being Spirit-led (write below):

Twelve Questions for Reflection

12. Of all that we can do in this life, do you rate anything higher than love?

Key scriptures:

> *This is my command: Love one another the way I loved you. This is the very best way to love. Put your life on the line for your friends. You are my friends when you do the things I command you.*
> John 15:12-14, MSG

> *If I speak in the tongues of men or of angels, but do not have love, I am only a resounding gong or a clanging cymbal. If I have the gift of prophecy and can fathom all mysteries and all knowledge, and if I have a faith that can move mountains, but do not have love, I am nothing. If I give all I possess to the poor and give over my body to hardship that I may boast, but do not have love, I gain nothing.*
> 1 Cor. 13:1-3, NIVUK

> *We love each other because he loved us first.*
> 1 John 4:19, NLT

For reflection:
Life can throw up a thousand distractions and our priorities can become skewed. We are all vulnerable to losing sight of what God considers to be most important. In the kingdom of God, love is the top priority. It is the first and second commandment: *Love God with all of your heart* and *Love your neighbour as yourself.* Indeed, all of the other commandments fall out of these two, so that love sums up the whole of God's law. This is not a law of scripted precepts; it's a law of life that needs to be imprinted directly

onto the human heart by the Spirit. Love for God comes from God, because he first loved us. He is the essence and fountainhead of love. Intimacy with the Lord awakens love in us; and the more we press into his loving presence, the more his love consumes us, spilling out to those around us.

Your own thoughts or prayer on love (write below):

Afterword for Those Affected by Book

If this book has stirred up any painful emotions when reading it, then I implore you not to sit on those feelings. The biggest mistake that I made in my life was neglecting my problems for too long, until the pain became unbearable and I had no choice but to seek help. My heart for you – and a primary motivation for writing this book – is that you would acquire help sooner rather than later. As such, I offer some advice here in the form of potential areas for you to consider and act on as follows:

- **Turn to God for help** – God is neither unconcerned nor incompetent in the matter of helping us. In fact, he is our best source of help, if we allow him to be such. Turn to him and give him scope to intervene in your life. Do not always seek instant change since you will be disappointed, though powerful, transformative encounters with God are always possible. God wants us to have a relationship with him. We need to hear his voice and let him speak peace to our hearts. This can happen through reading the Bible, talking to believers, listening to Christian sermons, using Christian resources (books, CDs, etc.), and even in unforeseen ways (Num. 22:28). This can be a whisper in the heart with the power to shift mountains – of shame, insecurity, anxiety, etc. God's words have the power to release us; but remember that restoration is a journey, not a quick fix.

- **Speak to someone you trust** – Hiding problems from others is damaging. Do not wait until your anxiety becomes an uncontrollable electrical storm inside you. My wife Lesley is my best friend and most trusted confidant in this earthly life. She may not be God, but her love and patience have shown me what the kindness of Christ looks like in action. Find someone who will listen to you without judgment. In turn, listen to them and do not dismiss what they have to say – our supporters often see things that we in our pain are oblivious to. My wife's straight-speaking has been a blessing, and I have learned the hard way that I cannot pull the wool over her eyes. We need to swallow our pride and let loved ones steer us in the right direction. (How precious were those words: 'Get to your GP before I lose the <expletive> plot!' Or words to that effect!)

- **Find a Spirit-led church** – The Holy Spirit is our teacher, comforter and guide in this present world. When he is welcomed as such in a church, that is somewhere you will want to be. It is a place where miracles can happen and where people can be restored back to life; not only through God's loving and restorative presence, but through the support of Spirit-led Christians who rely on God to minister effectively to others. The spiritual river needs to be flowing – indeed overflowing – with living water, and manifestly able to refresh and strengthen those who draw from it. You should feel deeply invigorated by church, not rendered comatose. Read the Book of Acts and tell me that church is not meant to be a powerhouse and charging station. I dare you! Church should be the talk of the town and not a byword for irrelevance. And remember, don't look for the perfect church: God's grace abounds in our weakness.

Afterword For Those Affected by Book

- **Get help, professional or non-professional, when necessary** – You will no doubt have sussed by now that I esteem the help of others, including doctors, counsellors, carers, friends and loved ones when necessary. In cases of profound or prolonged emotional crisis, I believe that key people are an integral part of God's intended recovery process for a person, while God himself is the definitive key to wholeness (spiritually, mentally and emotionally). Overlooking human intervention when it is vital and offered can be arrant nonsense; even dangerous. It reminds me of that well-known cautionary tale of the man who drowned and stood outside heaven's gates complaining to the gatekeeper that God was remiss in ignoring his prayers to be saved, only to be told that his foolish rejection of a lifeboat and a sea rescue helicopter, both sent by God, had been his undoing. Take the help on offer, while seeking God for that deeper inner release.

- **Use appropriate medication as directed by doctors** – My blood boils when I hear stories of well-meaning Christians instructing emotionally unwell people to come off their tablets and pray. It not only puts a heavy burden on people to perform their way out of illness, it is harmful. Pill-taking is not proof of unbelief or disobedience towards God, and when it serves to support an individual's recovery, it is good sense on a galactic scale. Take your tablets as directed by doctors – GPs or hospital doctors – and remain on them until advised otherwise. Moreover, when needing to discuss coming off medication, include loved ones in that conversation since our actions can have serious consequences for those around us. It may even be the case that we may require to be on medication for the rest of our natural lives. This should neither diminish the quality of our spiritual lives, nor undermine our status as fully accepted children of God. The Lord is unremittingly merciful, and our weakness and brokenness do not get in the way of that.

I leave you with the above suggestions and may God bless you on your journey into wholeness. Do not give up hope. My final word to you and one first articulated by the Apostle Paul:

God is for us and not against us!